HIGHWAYS AND BYWAYS OF BARNES

ACKNOWLEDGEMENT

The Barnes and Mortlake History Society gratefully acknowledge a generous donation from the Barnes Workhouse Fund which has contributed toward the cost of this publication.

HIGHWAYS AND BYWAYS OF BARNES

by
MARY GRIMWADE
and
CHARLES HAILSTONE

© Barnes and Mortlake History Society 1992
First published in 1992
by Barnes and Mortlake History Society
and
Picton Publishing (Chippenham) Limited
ISBN 0 948251 66 2

Set in Linotype Pilgrim by
Mike Kelly Phototypesetting,
Biddestone, Chippenham, Wiltshire SN14 7EA
Printed and Bound in the United Kingdom by
Picton Publishing (Chippenham) Limited
Queensbridge Cottages,
Patterdown,
Chippenham,
Wiltshire SN15 2NS
Telephone: (0249) 443430

CONTENTS

CONTENTS

LIST OF MAPS

LIST OF ILLUSTRATIONS

Front Cover: Railway Side and The Manor Arms looking West, 1976
Back Cover: A Barnes Lion

FOREWORD

It is a pleasure to be asked to write the foreword to a book about Barnes, the place where I live, and of which I am immensely fond. As its co-author Mary Grimwade notes in the introduction, this study is not meant to be a definitive history of Barnes; that has yet to be written. *Highways and Byways of Barnes* is in fact an affectionate appraisal of this most delightful corner of south-west London researched and written by two local historians who have known it all their lives.

The book is the result of many years of careful and painstaking study by the co-authors Mary Grimwade and the late Charles Hailstone. They have used both local and national primary sources and printed material, and have enlivened the text with their personal reminiscences. The reader is invited to explore the ancient fields, passages and footpaths, the waterways and ponds, and the green open spaces, which have over the centuries helped to shape the unique character of Barnes. Also discussed are the improvements to road transport and communications including the coming of the railways; the important enabling factors which were set to transform gradually a small quiet village into a pleasant suburb of London. It is, however, the large number of hitherto unrecorded aspects of Barnes which are at the heart of the book and which I believe will surprise even those who feel they know the place well.

The production of the book, the society's first major work on Barnes, has been dogged by delays, due largely to the unfortunate incapacity or illness of the co-authors. The final blow was the sudden death of Charles Hailstone in May 1991. Fortunately Mary Grimwade was determined that work on the book should go ahead. She faced a daunting task. A great deal of Charles Hailstone's work had been completed but a large amount remained at the rough note stage. With outstanding success Mary Grimwade has coped with both this and her own sections of the book. On behalf of the Barnes and Mortlake History Society, I offer her my sincere admiration and gratitude.

Charles Hailstone's enthusiasm for the projected book, which he himself described as 'a lovely subject', was a delight to behold. Whilst his heart was always in Mortlake, he had a sincere regard for neighbouring Barnes. His last work *Hammersmith Bridge* had proved to be an arduous undertaking, written as it was within the confines of a deadline. *Highways and Byways of Barnes* was different: the writing was to be a pleasure not a chore. I trust he would have approved of the completed book. I believe it to be a fitting tribute to the memory of a most complete local historian: a character who was as unique as Barnes itself.

MAISIE BROWN

INTRODUCTION

In no way at all does this book pretend to be a history of Barnes. The idea partly arose when chatting to the late Charles Hailstone about our early memories and how our later more detailed research had offered greater interest and depth to our reminiscences.

When Charles died, suddenly and unexpectedly, in May 1991 the manuscript was in hand but nowhere near completed. His family immediately passed on to the History Society his voluminous quantity of notes and photographs and, from then on, I applied myself to editing his work and combining my own, as we had originally agreed to divide the writing between us.

I am well aware that much material which we had both collected over many years of research is not included, but it was never our intention to include more than is covered by the title of the book. The Society is constantly in the process of adding to its publications, both in the form of the printed word and by illustrations, so we did not wish to repeat what has already been written. We had agreed to leave subjects which required more detailed treatment for future publications.

I feel I would have been unlikely to have completed this work after Charles's death had it not been for the unfailing support of the Publication Committee. I would here like, in this connection, to mention Richard Jeffree who, as suddenly as Charles, died at the end of 1991. He had remained a most regular attender at our meetings despite increasing ill health and even had a publication of his own in the process of writing at his death.

It is difficult to know whom to thank individually when so many people have given me their support. Firstly, I much appreciate the generosity of the Hailstone family in giving Charles's notes, papers, etc to the Society. The Staff of a variety of libraries, especially the Surrey Record Office and Richmond Reference Library, including that of the Local Collection, have never failed in their interest and co-operation. Mr David Catford, Mr Leslie Freeman, Mr Raymond Gill, Mrs Holmes, Mrs Norris and Dr David Redstone have provided photographs and illustrations from their personal collections as well as those acknowledged in the text. David Catford has my wholehearted thanks for the maps and plans which he has so patiently and ably reproduced and Mrs Maisie Brown has proof-read the typescript, and made many helpful suggestions.

In addition, generous donations in Charles's memory from a wide circle of his friends have been used towards the cost of the illustrations in this book. It is hoped that they will give added pleasure to the reader.

Even with all the unusual circumstances which have delayed the completion of this work I have felt some satisfaction in recording aspects of Barnes which might have been permanently lost. If it had not been for our research and personal memories I wonder how many people would have known where the Cattle Creep, the Icehouse or the Tadpole Pond were to be found.

MARY GRIMWADE

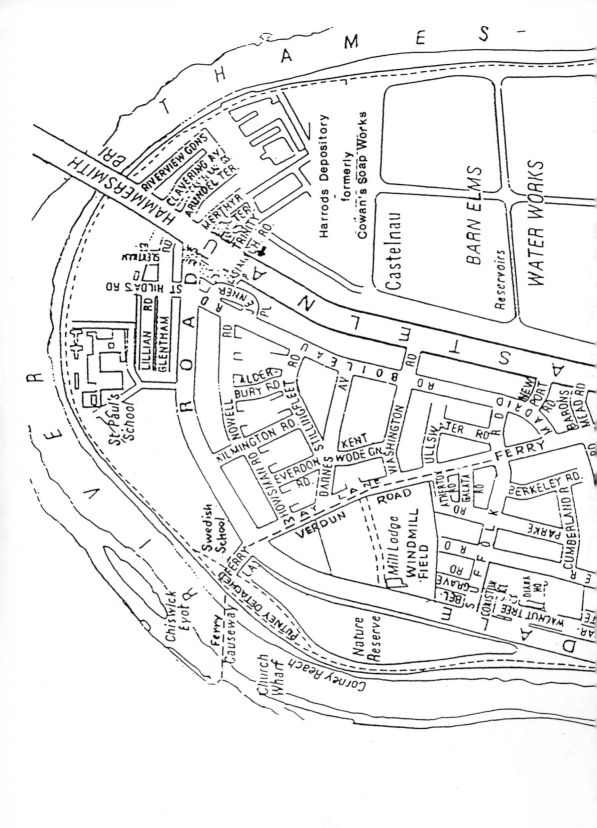

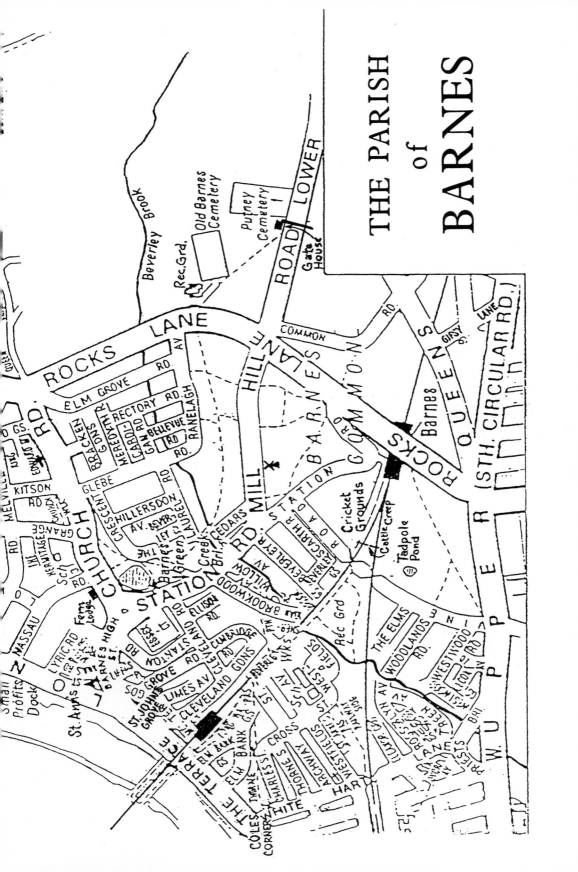

THE PARISH of BARNES

1. THE PARISH ENVIRONS

Barnes takes the shape of a duck's head, with the eye in Barn Elms and the beak pointing down towards Putney. It is surrounded on three sides by the great bend in the Thames which embraces Castelnau, Barn Elms and the village itself. The Beverley Brook in its furthermost reach is another water boundary. There was a stream on the west side of the White Hart Lane where Mortlake begins, and Barnes Common is parted from Putney by a mediaeval ditch, now dried up and overgrown. The old land boundaries are the Upper Richmond Road, Priests Bridge and Dyers Lane. For centuries the Lords of the Manor were the Dean and Chapter of St. Paul's Cathedral, Barnes having been given to them by King Athelstan, (925–940).

The highest point in Barnes is on Mill Hill, otherwise Roundhill, at 26.78 feet, but mostly it is low lying, much of it between 14 feet and 20 feet. On quitting the Common and leaving Barnes the ascent begins into the water bearing hills of Roehampton and the higher downs beyond. It is the abundance of water both flowing and below ground, the pond on the Green, the shallow valley of the Beverley Brook, the placid reservoirs, the sense of a high water table, the Common and the rurality of Barn Elms which give Barnes its immediately distinctive character. There is a freshness of air and grass of a brighter hue.

There were formerly many marshy areas, such as the Great More and Ireland, together with mediaeval drainage works and numerous ponds of which four were on or adjacent to the Green, with one remaining. Both the retiring course of the early Thames and the delta of the Beverley Brook left their mark beneath the top soil in the Castelnau peninsula. The whole of Westfields, the village and the church are on clayey brickearth. The Common is gravel with outcrops of sand and pebbles. In the past the moist land favoured the cultivation of exotics such as liquorice by the Beverley Brook, and of madder for crimson dye and hops at Barn Elms. It will thus be readily allowed that the waters of Barnes and the river bespoke the first settlement and the village which grew around it.

The Great More

There are archival references to an undefined area in the Northfield, the mediaeval open field in the Castelnau peninsula, to the Great More (1433), the Moor (1479) and Le Moore (1501), the name then appearing to lapse. It means marshy ground (cf morass). In 1441 Robert Lucas, the rector of Barnes, had an acre and a half of meadow there.

Ireland

Ireland is the old name for the wedge of residential roads extending northwards from Church Road to the Harrodian sports ground. The boundaries on its long sides are Grange Road – Parke Road and a line running along the back gardens on the western side of Byfeld Gardens northwards. The name has no connection with the Irish who worked in the market gardens of Barnes. It was recorded as Irland in 1489 and as Ilande and Yrland in 1519. By popular usage it was called Ireland throughout the nineteenth century.

The name denoted land in a marsh, so recalling the story that Barnes church was built on the edge of a marsh. The land was a dwindling place for the watercourse coming from the creek on the site of Hammersmith Bridge. Norton Lane (Grange Road) followed the firm edge of the ground which gave excellent meadow and pasture.

The southern part of Ireland was the Glebe land of Barnes, belonging to the parson, he and the church receiving all the profits and benefits from it, together with exemption from tithe. The northern part was divided into Middle Ireland and North Ireland. The Glebe land, then parted from the rest of Ireland by a line of mature trees, was developed as Westmoreland Road and Melville Road (1906), Kitson Road (1907) and Grange Road (1910). Lyttyll Irland, a close of five acres recorded in 1517, contains the northern half of Byfeld Gardens and the Melville Road cul-de-sac.

Development in the north of Ireland began with Suffolk Road in 1915, but most continued as arable land bearing crops until the making of Cumberland Road (1928), other roads, Galata Road (1938) and lastly Atherton Road.

The Castelnau Peninsula

The land contained in the great bend in the Thames, that is the Castelnau peninsula, including Barn Elms, presents an interesting geological study. Unlike that in similar bends upstream of Barnes it consists mainly of alluvium, apart from a wide swathe of gravel opposite Chiswick. The alluvium was deposited by the wide primaeval Thames and the delta of the Beverley Brook. Another contributor was a creek on the site of Hammersmith Bridge, which flowed into a watercourse going into the peninsula to the west of Boileau Road and Madrid Road. When the abutment for the first bridge was under construction in 1825 the creek flooded the works. A steam engine was brought on site. The creek was pumped out and filled in. Its old name lost, but it was then called Hoare's Sluice from the occupant of Barn Elms. The towing path crossing was Hoare's Bridge.

The Great and Little Works

In mediaeval times a double line of drainage ditches were dug parallel with the Thames from the end of the gravel opposite Chiswick church right round the river's bend and Barn Elms into the Beverley Brook. The towing path formed a causeway between the river and the Great Works. The Little Works of indeterminable length, presumably dug at a later time as a second line of flood defence, was separated from the Great Works by a strip of land of varying width much used for osier beds. The name comes from *weorc* in the sense of a defensive work, in this case to oppose flooding as a sump and so secure more land for pasture and arable use.

The Works occur in a rental of 1517:

> Itm of Thomas Oking and John Tollysworthe the elder and John Tollysworthe the younger for a twygghawe in the works betwixt the Temmes and the cross heyge in the lytill grove, the fyshing reserved for their lyves. Xs.

The cross hedge, also called the mark hedge, lay across the path of the Hammersmith Bridge approach road, now Castelnau, when it was laid out in 1825. A twighawe was an enclosure in which osiers were grown.

The Great and Little Works appear as reference points in the Barn Elms survey of 1649, for example:

> One pcell of Land planted wth Oziers Abbuttinge on the Workes on the South side, lyinge betweene that and Beverley Creeke conteyninge by Estimac(i)on 1 acre 2 roods.

Much of the system survived into the nineteenth century. A stretch of the Little Works appears on the 1867 OS 25in. as an unnamed length of water with a fringe of trees roughly between Clavering Avenue and Arundel Terrace. Part of the Great Works survived until after 1920 along the eastern edge of Barn Elms between the reservoirs and the Beverley to which it was admitted by a sluice. All that remains is the slight hollow inland of the towing path at that end of Queen Elizabeth Walk.

Barn Elms – The Manor House of Barnes stood on this site from earliest times. The mediaeval house was rebuilt in 1694 and wings added in 1770. It was demolished after a fire in 1954 having been in a bad state of repair for some time.

The earliest known view of Barnes Pond *circa* 1790. On the right of the group of buildings is the house known as Lowther Lodge (on the site of the present Barclays Bank). The next large building on the left is The Sun Inn. The cottage on the extreme left with the sharply pitched roof still stands and is at present a children's clothing shop.

Barnes Pond in the 1960's. 'Mary' and 'Bill' with their family of cygnets. This devoted pair of swans lived on the Pond for many years. Since their death, no swan has chosen to take up permanent residence on the Pond which otherwise supports a variety of waterfowl.

2. STILL WATERS PAST AND PRESENT

Barnes Pond

Most village ponds around London have gone and some places, including Mortlake, never had one. Barnes Pond is thus a rarity greatly cherished by the inhabitants and admired by visitors and artists who happen upon it. Ponds often occur in the angle of a crossroad where the highway has risen from constant mending to create a hollow to catch rain and storm water. At Barnes the bank is higher where the crossroads meet and here was the old hole in the pond. It will be noticed that The Crescent runs on a ridge and that the ground slopes downwards to the pond on that side. The pond may have formed as an overspill from the Beverley Brook and has been enlarged and dredged to provide a watering place for cattle, as it did into this century, or for stocking with fish.

Archival references to the pond are rare since it was merely sufficient for it to exist. There were formerly four ponds on or adjacent to Barnes Green, which was common land. The 1649 survey of the manor of Barnes records:

> The Royalties of Fishinge belonginge to the Lords of the Mannor of Two Ponds lyinge in the Comon of Barnes with two Ponds not graunted to any person but kept in theire owne hands and disposable are worthe beinge formerly lett 40s.

Cart Horses refreshing themselves in the Pond. The slope into the water was opposite the present Barclays Bank in Church Road.

The existing pond, once part of the glebe belonging to the Rector, was called the Great Pond or the Great Pool. The other three were the Little Pond or the Little Pool, the Long Pond and an unnamed pond, all noticed below.

Barnes Pond is a fraction above one and a half acres. The first reliable plan appears in James Taylor's map of 1783. It was then very much larger and of a pear shape, but with the flattened northern shore as of today. Its furthest extent southwards was to the broad footpath which crosses the Green to The Crescent. There is a dip in the level of the ground between the footpath and the bank of the pond, indicating the part which was filled in. Water was led in by a narrow rill, the stem of the pear as it were, from the Beverley. During a fair at Barnes in July 1802:

> Three Shropshire girls ran for a Holland shift, ornamented with Byng and Burdett's ribbands, round a pond a quarter mile in circumference, which was won by a girl about eighteen years old.

During the fruit picking season girls would walk up from Shropshire to work in the market gardens. The pond was reduced to its present size between 1825 and 1837.

Barnes Pond came near to destruction or severe spoliation by the Hammersmith Bridge Company which in 1824 obtained its Act for building the bridge and making approach roads. Plans were made and published for a road leaving the bridge south-westerly to enter Grange Road, go straight through the pond, into Westfields and come out at Priests Bridge in Mortlake. Dr. John Palin, an influential shareholder, who kept an academy for young gentlemen in Cleveland House overlooking the pond persuaded the Company to abandon the plan. In its stead the present Castelnau and the road across the Common were opened in 1827. Cleveland House north of the Methodist church was pulled down in 1927.

The extreme northern part of the pond was at one time parted from the rest by a line of white chains and posts to provide a watersplash for horses drawing carts in the summer. It was entered by a slipway opposite the Sun Inn and there was room for two wagons standing alongside. This rustic scene was a favourite subject for picture postcards, with the driver having a quiet pipe of tobacco on the box and the wheels up to the axletrees in the pond. The horses enjoyed the cooling water and very importantly the rims of the wooden wheels expanded against the iron tyres to restore a tight grip. Driving in and out of the watersplash needed some care. A horse stumbled and drowned whilst turning in 1902. The practice was forbidden by the Barnes Urban District Council in 1911, one reason being that hoofs were injuring the bed of the pond which had recently been coated with a thin layer of rough concrete. The watersplash and slipway were removed but to compensate the horses the BUDC applied to the Metropolitan Drinking Fountain & Cattle Trough Association for a water trough and fountain. This was given free by the Association in November 1911, the BUDC paying £12 for fixing it and laying on the water. It was sited 'between the pond and the Rhododendron Bed'.

A small circular island was made in the pond by 1837. Anderson wrote in 1900 that there was usually a pair of swans nesting upon it. Later the Vintners Company through its swan warden would sometimes present a pair to the BUDC, which had the care of the pond. The island was surrounded by a light iron railing with an opening for the swans. Cygnets were always removed to other waters or transferred to the Beverley. They were also given away or sold, as in 1900 when the keeper of Barnes Common was offered one pound for two, or thirty shillings for four.

The island was used in great public jubilations, as for the coronation of Edward VII in 1902, with special permission for the use of the pond's punt. For the coronation of George VI and Queen Elizabeth in 1937 a 'fountain of light' was put on the island. It was a low odeonesque pagoda illuminated at night with lights concealed in the eaves. A model galleon was moored in the pond. For these occasions, from the diamond jubilee of Queen Victoria onwards, the pond was ringed with coloured lanterns or fairy lights after dark.

The island was enlarged in 1975 and planted with a swamp cypress in 1976. During the blitz in the last war a bomb fell in the pond, creating another 'island' overnight.

Today the pond receives no natural supply of water, save from rain and land drainage. It is now replenished with mains water at an average 453,000 gallons a year. There was formerly an adjustable weir in the Beverley Brook a little downstream of the Cedars Road footbridge. It had three openings for letting down shutters on chains into the brook when needed for damming up the water which passed through a pipe under the Green and into the pond. The duty was performed by the Common keeper. The weir was a source of delight for children who would attempt a hazardous crossing, sometimes falling into the water. The weir is shown in many old picture postcards and photographs. It was removed in the 1960s and replaced by a pump housed in the square box-like concrete structure on the north bank of the brook upstream of the Cedars Road footbridge. The pump became ineffective and since the early 1970s no water from the brook has entered the pond. In 1893 a valve was inserted in the pond so that water could be used for flushing the sewers.

Fishing in the pond is prohibited because of injury to wildlife from lines and weights. However, during World War II the pond was stocked with fish in order to encourage those who were obeying the Government request to enjoy 'Holidays at Home' to find relaxation within familiar surroundings. The pond, which has a clay bed, is periodically drained for cleaning and the fish are removed to other waters. A few carp live in the pond. The dominant species are perch of small size. In April 1984, during the netting of the pond, a monster carp weighing fifteen pounds was removed. In the summer of 1970 an unsightly scum spread across the pond and it was said that the minnows which normally ate the algae had been devoured by pike which had found their way into the water.

The Long Pond This was a narrow spindle of water on the Little Green, between Church Road and The Crescent, on the west side of Glebe Road. The

This view of Barnes Church circa 1750 is of considerable interest. The Rectory had recently been rebuilt by the Revd. Francis Ware and the church wall is much as it is today. The elms at the far end had been planted in 1652 as recorded in the Church Register. The Long Pond is in the foreground and the inn at the extreme right is 'The Strugglers', rather misplaced by the artist but recognisible by its unusual roof.

site is marked by a pronounced hollow where the grass in hot dry summers retains its greenness and frosts linger in the winter. The ground here declines steeply from The Crescent. The pond appears in the Chatelain print of Barnes church from the west of 1750, with cattle browsing on its fringes. In 1797 the Long Pond was 'now filled up and paled in'.

The Little Pond Or the Little Pool. This was a smaller oval of water pointing north and south, below the south-east corner of Barnes Pond. It was filled in between 1837 and 1841. The southern arm of The Crescent runs across the site.

The name of the fourth pond on the Green is lost. It was a rectangle of water parallel with and a few steps from the Beverley to which it was connected. The straight sides suggest an artificial pond for cattle dipping or a sump when the Beverley was in spate. The site is a little downstream of the Cedars Road footbridge and south of Laurel Road.

The Railway Ponds

The gravel and earth used in making the embankments for the Rocks Lane overbridge in 1845 was taken from each side of the railway between Barnes station and Queen's Ride. The hollow filled with water to form the Railway ponds. Anderson recalled visiting them as a child:

About half a dozen of us schoolboys used to go there to fish on a half holiday, the only fish to be found being a very few roach and swarms of minnows and sticklebacks.

The ponds, the larger of the two being on the north side of the line, were filled in with spoil from the excavations for the Barn Elms reservoirs.

The Moat

Homestead moats might be made to prevent the wandering of cattle, to deter intruders, or as a symbol of prestige. The age of the Barnes example is not known. In the eighteenth century the 2a.2r.38p. within it was called the Moat Garden. This is exactly bounded by Willow Avenue, Brookwood Avenue, Station Road and Beverley Path. The moat shown on the Taylor map of 1783 consists of two arms of water forming a right angle. The southern arm was parallel with the Beverley Brook, from which it was parted by a narrow causeway to take the ancient Westfields footpath, now the brookside pavement of Willow Avenue. The other arm went northwards across Willow Avenue to the back garden wall between 30 and 32 Brookwood Avenue.

In 1740 the Moat Garden contained The Folly, later called Grove Cottage, perhaps deriving its name from the pronounced battlements along the front of the house. The land was then part of the Milbourne House estate. It was inherited by Joseph Partington in 1797. Miles Partington sold to the Baron Pierre Augustin de Noual and it followed through the Baroness to Patrick Adie. The moat was filled in between 1825 and 1837.

James Nichols, the builder of The Lion Houses, was in 1906 given leave to develop the Grove House Estate with its pleasant garden and walks. He built nineteen houses on the north side of Brookwood Avenue and others in Willow Avenue. He had earlier built the six larger houses on the Station Road frontage, hence the three Nichols Lions on the Willow Avenue flank wall. Willow Avenue and Brookwood Avenue, as first built, were reduced to rubble in the blitz by a landmine which fell on the night of 25 September 1940.

Tagg's Yard Moat

A narrow ring moat connected by a stem of water to the Beverley Brook appears on a plan of 1836 in what is now the back garden of Tagg's Yard, off Woodlands Road. Its origin, either as an enlargement of a small cattle pond or as a fancy, is not known. The outside diameter was about one hundred feet. The moat surrounded a grass island. The field containing the moat ran south-east to a lane, now Vine Road. In the 1865 OS The Woodlands (12 Vine Road) is standing and there is a miniscule footbridge crossing the moat on the south side to the island which is planted with shrubs. With the development of Woodlands Road, named from The Woodlands or the nearby Woodlands Villa, the remains of the moat were filled in. The ring of the moat is now marked by a circular garden path. Tagg's Yard was named from Thomas Tagg who kept the Woodlands Riding Stables there between the wars.

The Waters of Barn Elms

Only a fingertip of the lake at Barn Elms has survived the demolition of the mansion in 1954 and the laying out of the grounds as a wide and airy expanse of school playing fields and sports centre. Here there are broad green prospects with unbroken lines of trees against the horizon and owls and foxes come out at night. In addition to the lake there were ponds, short canals and other water features connected by sluices to the Beverley Brook which was tidal at this point and to the Thames. Along the waterside edge ran the Great Works, the drainage ditch of mediaeval origin.

Barn Elms preserves the Saxon name of Barnes in the singular form. The last of the venerable elms perished in the disease of the late 1970s, but there is welcome evidence of some regeneration and new resistant plants are thriving with vigour. The general history of Barn Elms and its residents is not within the scope of this study. In the manorial survey of 1649 the house is described as 'beinge partly built with Brick partly built with Tymber commonly called Barn Elmeshouse' and there was a large orchard 'well planted wth Foure Fishe Pondes therein'. An advertisement of 1659 spoke of 'spring water brought to the house in leaden pipes' suggesting a service from the conduit on Barnes Common.

From the cluster of cottages and outbuildings at one time around it Barn Elms has been likened to a hamlet of the village of Barnes, with Barn Elms Lane leading from the main entrance down to the big house. The house was rebuilt in 1694, two wings were added in 1771 and it remained much in that form to the end. The estate included the house and grounds and the whole of the great northern bend in the river, with farms amidst the hedged fields and meadows. The Hammersmith Bridge Company was obliged to purchase the entire estate for the sake of the six linear acres needed to make its Surrey approach road, now Castelnau. Having opened the first suspension bridge in 1827 the Company sold the mansion and estate for market gardens, reservoirs and houses as opportunity afforded.

On removing from Fulham in 1884 the Ranelagh Club took a long lease on Barn Elms from the Ecclesiastical Commissioners. This lasted until 1939 and when the Club closed down a proposal was made by the company which had gained posses-sion of the land to build an estate of flats but to retain the mansion. This plan was thwarted by the outbreak of war shortly after. The mansion was requisitioned for the Services. On vacation after the war it became an object of vandalism. It was burnt out in 1954 and demolished as a dangerous structure. The site is now covered by The Wilderness, a dense spinney north of the running track. Brick remnants trace the foundations amongst the wild undergrowth.

The Lake   Occupying together with its island a little over three acres the lake reached its final form in 1771, when the lessee of Barn Elms, Richard Hoare, later knighted, laid out the grounds. Other water features were extended or newly created such as the Long Canal parallel with the Beverley Brook. The ornamental heritage was described by Cyril Fitzgerald in 1913 when one could.

by standing close to the sluice that regulates the lake, see a land and water

Still Waters in Barn Elms in the Spring of 1939. This lake has now been filled in and the ground is used as a running track.   With acknowledgements to *Times Newspapers Ltd.*

scape that would be hard to match and impossible to beat within the same
distance from London. It is not the sight alone, incomparable though it be,
that offers itself to the eye. There is, to the imaginative mind, something
very beautiful, something very solemn in the stillness, peace and repose of
the spot.

Since fish, either fresh, dried or salted, was an important part of the mediaeval
and later diet, the lake provided a ready larder for Barn Elms, supplemented by
those kept in the stew ponds. The Lake is marked as a fish pond as late as the
1952 25in. OS.

Sir Lancelot Shadwell (1779–1850) the lawyer and last Vice-Chancellor of
England, who lived at Barn Elms from 1827, was also the president of the
Society of Psychrolutes whose members were required to bathe out of doors
daily between November and March. He was fond of bathing in the lake and one
day when a party of lawyers, barristers, registrars, solicitors and clerks arrived
unexpectedly to obtain an important injunction, conducted business whilst up
to his chin in the water. The lake was the scene of a tragedy when a son of his
was drowned whilst rowing an outrigger, then newly invented, which became
entangled in water weeds and capsized.

In 1948 a notice of compulsory purchase by Surrey County Council and the
London County Council led to the infilling of the lake. It was done with clinker

from the extensive heaps at the Council dust destructor at Mortlake between the river and Kew Meadows Path. Filling began in 1957 and by April the next year lorries had deposited 19,217 tons in the lake. The dust destructor closed in 1962. The main central sheet of water is now covered by the running track. The extreme north finger of the lake remains and is fished by the Barnes and Mortlake Angling Club. The denizens include carp, perch, rudd, roach and tench. The water, silent within a border of tall crowding trees, can be glimpsed from Queen Elizabeth Walk.

The Reservoirs

The Barnes reservoirs were created by the old West Middlesex Water Works Company (WMWW). Marked by a tall chimney visible for many miles around, the works were on the Hammersmith side of the river near the western end of the Upper Mall and came into operation in 1808. Water was pumped direct from the adjacent Thames until 1838 when the intake was moved upstream to a point off Barnes Terrace. The increasing need for storage and the demand for settling reservoirs led to the purchase of land on the Barnes bank from the Hammersmith Bridge Company in 1828. The earliest Barnes reservoir, long and narrow, hugging the towing path, is covered by the western playing fields of St. Paul's school. It was later to be called the East Reservoir, or No. 1.

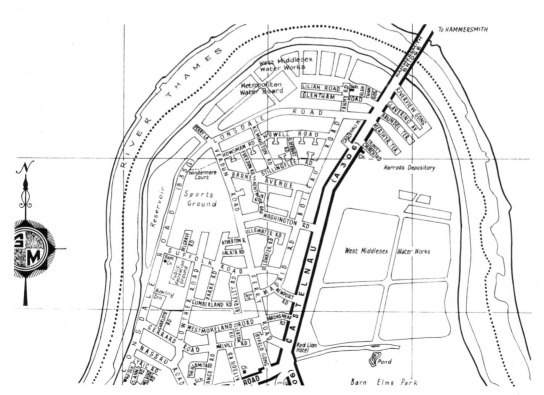

BARNES RESERVOIRS: This map shows the site of the reservoirs prior to the building of St. Paul's and the Swedish Schools.

In 1830 the WMWW acquired West Mead, a mediaeval meadow from the Dean and Chapter of St. Paul's for a second reservoir. This was called the West Reservoir, or No. 2, the division between the two being the path to Chiswick Ferry. Both came into use by 1838 when a Boulton & Watt beam engine in the Hammersmith works pumped the water through a 30in. iron pipe under the river. The West Reservoir was enlarged to twenty-two acres in 1879. It was discontinued in 1960 and narrowly eluded development for housing. Known from its shape as the Leg of Mutton the defunct reservoir is closely hemmed in with trees and hawthorn and holly hedges, forming the Barnes wildlife sanctuary between the towing path and Lonsdale Road.

Because of increasing river pollution from riparian industry, paddle steamers and the spread of the metropolis the WMWW was obliged by law from 1855 not to take water from the Thames below Teddington. A pumping station was built at Hampton which started sending water to the Barnes reservoirs in July 1855. What came to be known as the Barnes Water Works now expanded, a number of filter beds being laid down from 1854 onwards. By 1862 No. 3 Reservoir was made on the south side of the East Reservoir. The grassy banks remain alongside the railings at Lonsdale Road, with perfectly flat playing fields on the top of the reservoir.

Despite all this water near to hand the WMWW's first piped supply to Barnes did not come until 1866 when a service was laid on for a hundred or so dwellings in the rapidly developing Westfields. Previously and until the WMWW and its competitors supplied the whole parish with water, Barnes people depended on shallow wells, rain butts and hand pumps. By 1882 the complex of filter beds and reservoirs occupied the crescent of the Thames for a mile and a quarter south-westwards from Hammersmith Bridge. Most is now covered by St. Paul's school, opened in September 1968, and its grounds and playing fields. The old iron perimeter railings with unclimbable spikes remain along the riverside and in Lonsdale Road and Castelnau.

Hammersmith Bridge Reservoir   Otherwise No. 4 Reservoir, now gone, was a fine sheet of water which stretched northwards from a few paces inside the railings alongside Castelnau at its approach to the bridge. Between its northern edge and the river were six filter beds. Passers by and people on buses could thus enjoy a waterscape with lines of trees against the horizon. Seven and a quarter acres in extent and holding twenty-four million gallons this reservoir gave the impression of a lake, sparkling in the sun, but decidedly choppy in the winter, although the banks were designed to break rolling waves and prevent eroding spray. About halfway along the Castelnau edge was an intriguing sort of reverse whirlpool rising slightly above the surface at the point where water was constantly pumped up from beneath into the reservoir. All this visual attraction ceased with the emptying and infilling of the reservoir in 1965. The site is now occupied by the beautifully kept eastern playing fields of St. Paul's school.

The reservoir came into use in 1882 but the previous history of the land is curious. It was first purchased by the WMWW from the Hammersmith Bridge

Company in 1828, but abandoned and sold off in 1834. In the 1867 25in. OS the whole of the land between the river and Castelnau and the backs of Lillian Road and Glentham Road is marked for a housing development which would have entirely changed the riverside aspect here. In 1862 four streets were marked on a plan by the Metropolitan Freehold Building Society. The two longest streets were to be River Terrace alongside the towing path to join Castelnau, and Barnes Grove (otherwise Lansdowne Road) at the back of Lillian Road and Glentham Road. These two streets were to be connected at their western ends by West Road and by Lyndhurst Road which would have been in line with Fanny Road (now St. Hilda's Road). Altogether there would have been 131 houses, with a tavern provided. As it happened the need for expansion by the WMWW obliged it to repurchase the land and instead of houses the Hammersmith Bridge Reservoir and filter beds were constructed.

The mains from the Barnes works to the Hammersmith works, laid in 1838 and 1870, were replaced in 1898 by a tunnel of 7ft. 3in. in diameter. It was driven through the London clay at a depth of 50 ft. feet by means of a Greathead shield. The myth of an old secret passage under the river from Barnes to Hammersmith is thus disposed of.

Barn Elms Reservoirs The four huge squarish sheets of water lying between Castelnau and the river, bounded on the south by Queen Elizabeth Walk, dominate the map of the Castelnau peninsula. The reservoirs are hidden from view by houses, trees and tall embankments. They form a trapezium divided into quarters by grassed causeways. At the northern end are five filter beds which were served by a railway for a travelling crane. The reservoirs occupy 18¼, 20¼, 23¾ and 24¼ acres and were constructed to hold 73, 82, 96 and 99 million gallons respectively. In recent years the maximum depth of water was 15¾ft., containing a variety of fish and frequented by wildfowl including tufted duck, pochard, shoveller and smew. Together with the allotments north of the filter beds the area is 140 acres in extent. The land when mostly market gardens was leased to the WMWW by the Dean and Chapter of St. Paul's in 1894. Excavation and construction with brick linings began in 1895 and the reservoirs were completed within two years. The greatest number of workmen employed on the works at any one time was about 850. Some of the spoil was used to fill in the Railway Ponds by Barnes station. Barn Elms Farm was submerged in the course of the works.

The Metropolis Water Act was passed in 1902 when the supply of water from the Barnes Works stood above 22 million gallons daily. The Metropolitan Water Board absorbed the WMWW in 1904. The controlling authority is now Thames Water. When the London Water Ring Main comes into operation the reservoirs will be redundant and there is a proposal to create a Wildfowl and Wetlands Trust centre on the site.

3. RUNNING WATERS PAST AND PRESENT

The Beverley Brook and The Rythe

The Beverley Brook which flows through Barnes to empty into the Thames at the boundary of Barn Elms with Putney is said to derive its name from the beavers sought for their fur which throve along its banks. The name compares with Beversbrook in Wiltshire (Beversbroc in 1086) meaning 'beaver stream' and with Beverley in Yorkshire. Since *ley* is cognate with *stream* the Beverley Brook is in effect a double name. No early form has been found. A brookside meadow called Beverey Mede is recorded in 1548. It is Beverley Creeke in 1649 and Baveley Brook on a map of 1822. It secures permanence as the Beverley Brook in the 1865 OS. There are a few references to it as a river in the last century and later.

In a rental of 1516 the Beverley is the *creke*. The rustic title persisted locally and there are many older inhabitants who continue to call it the Creek. Creek Bridge is in fact the proper name for the Station Road bridge. There was a third name, the Beverley being called the Common Shore (or sewer) at Mortlake in 1618 and intermittently at Barnes, also in reports to the old Metropolitan Board of Works (1855–1889). The description of sewer was originally applied to a natural watercourse.

The Beverley rises in Cuddington in Surrey, half a mile south-west of Worcester Park railway station, six and a half miles crow fly south of its confluence with the Thames at Barn Elms. Because of meanderings the stream length is eight miles. Much of the course can be followed by foot. It is initially a chalk stream, gathering its head waters from the Surrey foothills at Banstead Downs. Piped beneath a housing estate the Beverley first emerges in a concrete culvert on the north side of Central Road. The infant brook then flows between grassy banks and hawthorns. Some seventy per cent of the water in the Beverley is harmless effluent, without which there would be little movement.

At Beverley Park the Beverley receives its major tributary, the Pyl Brook, here of the same width. Thus refreshed the Beverley skirts Malden golf course where it accepts the Coombe Brook taking its rise in the heights to the west. Next it is lost beneath the Coombe Lane-Kingston Bypass intersection. It reappears in a wide valley in a well wooded and thicketed course alongside Wimbledon Common, from whence it accepts the meagre offerings of the Farm Ravine, the Stag Bog Ditch and the Glen Albyn.

The Beverley enters Richmond Park at Robin Hood. A little before the bridge near Roehampton Gate it is joined by the Hartington Brook, a Mortlake stream which descends from the Pen Ponds. Quitting the park it runs on the east side of Palewell Fields and the Hertford Avenue allotments, thence under Priory Bridge and The Willoughbys. It enters Barnes proper on the east side of Priests Bridge. Looking over the parapet the White Hart Lane culvert is seen delving into its tunnel under the Halfway House to the north. The culvert operates when water overtops the lip at its entrance. In spates or heavy storms the sight and sound is tumultuous. The culvert runs beneath White Hart Lane to empty into the Thames at Mortlake, a few steps west of White Hart Alley. (See also The Culverts.)

Priests Bridge is an ancient name. It was Prestbrig in 1479 and Prists Brig in 1518. Rustic corruptions occur from the eighteenth century onwards as Peace Bridge, Piece Bridge and Peas Bridge, sometimes on maps. These forms were still used by some of the older inhabitants fifty years ago. The name is thought to come from the passage of the priests between Wimbledon and Mortlake.

Until the Upper Richmond Road was rerouted across Priory Bridge by The Willoughbys in 1930 it passed over Priests Bridge which carried all the buses and traffic. The Putney boundary was moved to the middle of the road between the bridge and the Upper Richmond Road in 1957, having previously run behind the neat foursquare double cottages on the north-east side. These cottages were standing by 1827 and in No. 2, fronting the Upper Richmond Road was established the early Putney police station. On the north-east parapet of the bridge is a metal plate dated 1904:

> Any person sticking bills or committing any other nuisance or in any way defacing or damaging this bridge will be prosecuted.

On entering Westfields the Beverley is soon lost to view when it veers north-west between the back gardens of Treen Avenue and Woodlands Gardens. On the southerly bank between Westwood Road and Woodlands Road the brook watered a small ring moat (see Tagg's Yard Moat). The plain flat footbridge connecting Woodlands Road and Rosslyn Avenue was opened in 1963 to avoid a previously tiresome detour.

Whilst the Beverley continues to take a meandering course its more pronounced bends were removed to secure a better flow. In Mediaeval times meadows and osier beds were formed and continued into the last century in the spurs of land within these half loops. The largest was a bow some 300ft. across its neck, on the southerly bank between Woodlands Road and under the railway to the Vine Road recreation ground. This was in 1433 recorded as *le brodehooke*, the Broad Hook, when the lords of the manor and the underbailiff were before the homage court for failing to keep hogs out of the meadow there. Its title long forgotten the Broad Hook appears on a plan of 1881, when a new road then unnamed was proposed to cut into it. This is now Woodlands Road. The Beverley was subsequently diverted across the neck of the hook, save the turn north under the railway.

Between the two railway lines the Beverley ripples along the edge of the Vine Road recreation ground behind a line of trees. The recreation ground occupies the greater part of a pasture known as Island into the decline of the last century. It was recorded as Elond in 1461. The name of Old English provenance was then already ancient, meaning land by the *ea* or stream. In 1519 it was Ilande, 'buttyng northe and southe upon the heythe'. The Heath was the usual name for

The footbridge across Beverley Brook. To the right can be seen the weir which could be raised or lowered to control the flow of water. The name Beverley School is on the fence which surrounded the large house hidden in the trees. This is now the site of Beverley Close.

Barnes Common. Other variants were Elandes (1523) and Ealands (19c). The north-west part of Island lies under the loop line. The south-east boundary was a lane, now Vine Road. Alexander Barker of East Sheen and Walter Barker of Barnes, market gardeners, became the tenants of Island in 1882. It was an orchard when five acres of the land were bought by the Barnes Urban District Council in 1929 to lay out as the Vine Road recreation grounds.

Between the back of the Westfield Flats and the north-east bank of the Beverley was Liquorish Close, a long narrow tract mentioned in 1751. Here the licorice or sweetroot was cultivated. The plant grows to four feet with whitish purple flowers. A rub oil was extracted from the roots and a soothing balm for catarrh and sore throat.

Passing under the loop line of 1849 the brook flows through Sheridan Place. The name for the part between the brook and Beverley Path in the Victorian era was Goslings. Osiers grew on the edge of the brook. The Beverley takes a short turn to the north in Sheridan Place and resumes its north-westerly course alongside Willow Avenue. Here the long fronds of water plants trail with the current.

Station Road crosses the Beverley on Creek Bridge. Until the first bridge was built all wagons, horses and cattle had to go through a wide watersplash or ford, with a very narrow footbridge on the north-west side. In September 1792 the Barnes vestry invited tenders for a brick bridge. The only tender, that of John Mitchell for £97.19s. was duly accepted. To avoid a special rate on the inhabitants a subscription list was opened. The contributors included:

Sir Richard Hoare of Barn Elms, £20.

Lady Hoare, the Dean and Chapter of St. Paul's cathedral (Lords of the Manor), John Waring (Bulls Head), Charles Rix, George Chapman, Joseph Blizard and William Blizard, 5gns. each.

Admiral Stanton (Milbourne House), John Mitchell (builder) and Samuel Gatward (Rising Sun), 2gns. each.

William Bolton, Richard Wilson, Samuel Watson, William Rain, Henry Heyman, William Baker, Nathaniel Sprigg, Elizabeth Hunt and Fras. Waring, 1gn. each.

Mr Mitchell's bill was £145.16s. for the bridge and £16.9s.6d. for the railings. The walls were 4ft. 6in. high and 14in. thick. It was slightly humped with two arches to take the Beverley, approached from both sides by wooden posts and handrails and about 9ft. wide. The present Creek Bridge is a dull flat structure of brick and concrete, but with some slight remnants of the previous bridge on the underside.

The most familiar and picturesque stretch of the Beverley runs between the Green and the Common. Railings part it from the path at the bottom of Cedars Road. The willows which ornament the opposite bank were planted in 1925. The Cedars Road footbridge is very much a tarrying place for children and those out for a stroll. Barnes Pond was once replenished by an open stream from the brook at this point. Here there is a concrete sluice to help the flow of the brook which develops a pleasing ripple above a clear bed of sand and pebbles, but it shortly disappears from view as it bears north-westerly between Laurel Road and the end of Glebe Road. There it formed a fork with the Rythe which picked its way along the edge of the Common (see The Rythe). In the great drought of 1976 when all about was sear a line of brighter grass marked its course into the Beverley. The confluence of the two watercourses shows in the ground here.

Before the ground from Glebe Road to Rocks Lane was built over, from 1896 the Beverley rippled between meadows and pastures. On the south side between it and the Rythe was the Moormead, lush and green, bordered with trees and bushes. From the northern bank the old Town Long Croft, a large field of fourteen acres stretched towards Church Road with a lone tree in its midst. Its other name was the Great Summer Field, conjuring thoughts of buttercups and long golden days. The eastern boundary is marked by the back garden fences between Rectory Road and Elm Grove Road. From thence to Rocks Lane was the six acre Pond Mead.

In the estate there are glimpses of the brook as it threads between back gardens and the tall confining walls of the houses. Each of the four roads is carried across a bridge in keeping with the architecture of the estate. All have end piers in brick and terracotta, some surmounted by globes, and interlacing ironwork parapets. On the west side of the Bellevue Road bridge old maps show a narrow cattle bridge connecting the Great Summer Field with the Moormead. A sad tale attaches to the brook between the Rectory Road and Elm Grove Road bridges. In January 1911 an inquest sat upon the body of Antonio Paganuzzi, a kitchen porter found drowned in twelve inches of water.

The earlier Rocks Lane bridge was humped with a single arch. Before the lane was made up across the Common in 1827 it petered out into a cart track on the other side of the brook. Emerging on the east side of the flat and unromantic road bridge the Beverley at once pursues a quiet and countrified course at Barn Elms. There is the Long Meadow, a mediaeval survival, well sprinkled with daisies between it and the relict Rythe on the northern edge of the Common. Here the bank is tall, having been built up in 1958 to contain floods, smothered in white cow parsley and crowded with trees and hawthorns aslant the water. At the eastern end of Barn Elms there was, in the survey of 1649, a timber bridge called Barnes Bridge 'passing from the Towne to Puttney'. The Putney boundary is marked on the south side of the brook by an iron link fence at the east end of the Long Meadow.

From near here the brook had a series of small tight windings or hooks, taken out in the last century to help the flow. On the Putney Lower Common bank the brook is concealed by forbidding thickets of brambles and bushes. Two flat concrete bridges cross to Barn Elms where there is a narrow earth footpath, parted from the brook by tangled bushes and trees, which runs along opposite Horne Way to come out on the Thames towing path.

The last quarter mile or so was formerly tidal with sluices to supply the waters of Barn Elms. To avoid tidal back floodings the basin at Ashlone Wharf was constructed in the 1970s. On reaching this point the Beverley, having drained fifteen square miles together with its tributaries, expands into a silent lagoon behind a thick fringe of trees. The penned waters enter the basin through an adjustable sluice and so into the Thames. The towing path is carried across on a brick and iron bridge at the end of the Beverley's eight mile journey.

Eel Fair

In 1905 the Bishop of Calcutta, a native of Barnes and a son of the rector, the Rev. E. Copleston, recalled catching eels in the Beverley Brook as a child. Earlier the eagerly awaited event was Eel Fair, beginning in May, about the tenth day. Immense numbers of young eels came up the Thames from the sea, turning into riverside creeks on the way. At Barn Elms the eels entered the Beverley, travelling through Barnes and Mortlake into Richmond Park. East of the carriageway near Roehampton Gate the eels turned into its Mortlake tributary, the Hartington Brook, which they ascended to congregate in the Pen Ponds in vast shoals. People could scoop them by the pailful.

The phenomenon declined after 1860 and largely disappeared by 1890. Writing in 1842 Edward Jesse, the naturalist, said the eels were about two inches in length, coming up the Thames in 'one regular and undeviating column of about five inches in breadth, and as thick together as it is possible to be' for between two and three days. An occasional eel is still found in the Beverley.

The Culverts

As estates developed in the upstream drainage territory of the Beverley Brook its course in Barnes became increasingly overburdened in storms and winter thaws. Flooding was seasonal in Station Road, the Green, Barn Elms and the streets in between. Picture postcards show children paddling in unaccustomed places and vehicles braving the swirling waters. The first proposal for a stormwater culvert from the Beverley Brook at Priests Bridge to the Thames was abandoned on the outbreak of the Great War in 1914. The Culvert Bill was passed by Parliament as a matter of urgency in 1923.

Following the letting of contracts White Hart Lane was to present a remarkable spectacle. The road was taken up and a deep trench excavated along its length and across its width, the chasm being revetted with stout timbers and flying buttresses. A railway was laid along the Barnes side for travelling steam cranes and wagons to remove the spoil and bring the concrete mixed in an adjoining street. The digging was manual in stiff yellow clay. By agreement much of the labour was locally recruited to ease unemployment. Tunnellers bored beneath the level crossing so that trains could run without interruption. The concrete culvert was completed and White Hart Lane restored in December 1927 at a cost of £42,057.9s.4d. Barnes contributed £8,000. The Thames outfall is in Mortlake, a few paces west of White Hart Alley.

Within a few years further developments in Raynes Park, West Barnes, Malden and Worcester Park brought the need for a relief culvert at Barnes. It was made from the Beverley near the Vine Road recreation ground to the Thames just west of Barnes Bridge. Work began in 1937 from both ends and under Elm Bank Gardens. Mechanical excavators were used and a small petrol locomotive with wagons ran on a light railway to serve the works.

The Rythe

The Rythe was filled in around 1904 when its name had long since lapsed. It rose on Putney Lower Common, taking a course westwards and mostly parallel with the Beverley Brook. It provided a natural boundary for Barn Elms and the northern edge of Barnes Common, emptying into the Beverley behind the southern end of Glebe Road. The name was recorded in 1433 as *le ryth*, meaning a little stream.

The old fork of the Rythe and the Beverley is discerned in the lay of the ground where the latter turns sharply north-east between Laurel Road and the bottom of Glebe Road. A few tall old willows mark the defunct course. Here both streams were of the same width. The back garden walls of 44–54 Glebe Road and 30–32 Ranelagh Avenue exactly follow the north bank of the Rythe. The latter two houses stand in a bend of the Rythe. Behind them is a wild tangle of twisted trees, brambles and dense bushes. This was a watercress bed in the latter years of the Rythe and two springs continue to assert themselves. At each step water bubbles up amongst the tufts of coarse grass.

Leaving the marsh, whose isolation ensures a good showing of bluebells, the stream bed is responsible for the damp and gloomy hollow of tall spreading trees, thorns and stinging nettles between the Common and Ranelagh Avenue. The glade passing through it is often wet and muddy, evidence of the relict Rythe running below. Two contributory springs came out of the bank on the southern side with the vanished conduit house between them. On the east side of Rocks Lane, then carried over it on a humped brick bridge, the Rythe watered a marsh in the purlieus of the tennis courts. It dwindled thence into a narrow stream between steep banks, traces of which remain amongst the forest trees on the edge of the Common. The Rythe was filled in following complaints that it smelt nastily, did not drain the Common, and served as a sink for flood water from the Beverley when in spate.

The Rustic Bridge This took the footpath from opposite 10 Ranelagh Avenue across the Rythe to the Common and Mill Hill. A quaint wooden bridge with lattice work of rough branches for the parapets it provided a favourite postcard view in the picturesque fashion.

The Conduit

The Conduit or conduit house, properly pronounced *cundit*, on Barnes Common stood on the south bank of the Rythe a few steps west of the footpath leading from opposite 10 Ranelagh Avenue to Mill Hill. It was a collection place for spring water. In the seventeenth century spring water was conveyed to the manor house at Barn Elms in leaden pipes. Anderson had a print of the remains of a brick water works on Barnes Common. In the Chatelain *South View of Barnes* (c1750) above a fold in the ground representing the banks of the Rythe there is a small square building, with an opening in each wall, angle pilasters and a flat roof, but the depiction is suspect since the print displays many inaccuracies. A reliable drawing of 1802 shows a low brick barrel vault to cover the deep cistern for collecting the water. The Conduit is mentioned in 1739 and appears in the 1865 25in. OS.

The water having filtered through the gravel of the Common was much esteemed. There is a charming reference in *Bits About Barnes*, a small penny pamphlet, now very scarce, published by Will Winch, the landlord of the White Hart, in 1894:

> On the northern side of the Common, close to the road leading to
> Hammersmith, is a spring of water which is famous for its clearness and
> purity. It is almost as noted as the well of St. Winifred and all sorts and
> conditions come there to drink the water. Children have been cured of
> weak eyes by its efficacy; teetotallers swear by it and boating men have
> been known to carry their whisky from the White Hart on purpose to
> adulterate it therewith. The doctors say it is so pure that only *animalculae*
> of the very lowest vitality can exist in it.

A spring on either side of the Conduit delivered a rill of water to the Rythe. In 1899 a rockery was formed round the outlet of what was then called the *Little*

Spring. The water was piped up in 1904. It is not known when the Conduit was built or taken down. No traces seem to exist in the lumpy bank on the site, at least above ground.

The Moormead   In 1517 the land between the Rythe and the Beverley which contains Ranelagh Avenue (1897) and ends of the roads leading off it was recorded as the *greate moremead* and the *litille moremead*. The name means marshy meadow and is a common one (cf the Great More in the Castelnau peninsula and The Moormead by the River Crane at St. Margarets). The boundary between the two meadows is now the back alley between Rectory Road and Elm Grove Road. After the conduit was built on the Common the Little Moormead was itself divided into two. The part abutting on Rocks Lane was called Conduit Mead by 1741. In 1908 it was described as an 'unsightly swamp' and filled in. The way into the Moormead was a farm bridge crossing the Beverley from the Great Summer Field on the west side of Bellevue Road. The meadowland continued on the east side of Rocks Lane in Barn Elms where an unspoilt mediaeval meadow, the Long Meadow, remains between the Beverley and the defunct Rythe.

The Rustic Bridge over The Rythe circa 1903. It gave access to Barnes Common from a point opposite No. 10 Ranelagh Avenue.

22

4. THE PASSAGES AND FOOTPATHS OF BARNES

One of the delights in exploring Barnes is the discovery of the passages which are hidden amongst the back streets of Westfields. There is a curiously enclosed and intimate air about them, with long picturesque vistas of old walls and cottages ornamented by miniscule front gardens full of flowers in the summer and here and there verdant canopies offering shade from above. Where paths cross and shoot off in various directions or dive into tunnels under the railway embankment there is a momentary impression of the labyrinth for the visitor. It should always be remembered that until the development of Westfields in the latter half of the nineteenth century all were open footpaths through the fields and market gardens. A similar system of paths in the other rural half of Barnes, north-east of the High Street, was gradually covered by estates from the first decade of the present century.

The paths, as did those now gone, pursue courses laid down many centuries ago and so continue in everyday use as the earliest remaining works of ancient times. They were trodden into being as the shortest or most convenient way from one point to another, either by travellers between distant places and traders with packhorses, or by the villagers working in the fields and meadows or making for the church. The need for the local paths arose as the mediaeval open fields were created and extended on both sides of the village as the West Field and the North Field. Modern dedications are very rare. Queen Elizabeth Walk along the northern edge of Barn Elms was opened in 1972.

Rights of way have always been carefully watched. The closure or impediment of a path or highway was for generations the concern of the villagers through the vestry and the manorial court, often with proceedings at law. The manifold administrative strands were brought together in an Act of 1800, strengthened by the Highways Act of 1835, to which many of the highways in this study were subject. It was laid down that an established path was a highway as much as a lane or street. The diversion or stopping up, otherwise closure, of a highway required an order and certificate from two magistrates as it continues so to do. A copy of an application and the reasons for it had to be published in a newspaper, affixed to the door of Barnes church for four Sundays and posted at each end of the highway concerned.

Two magistrates would view the highway and if thought fit would make an order and issue a certificate for enrolment, subject to any appeal by aggrieved parties. The common reasons for stopping up or diversion were that the path or highway was not much used, ill kept, choked with weeds, impassable with mud in wet weather, a lurking place for misdemeanour, an encroachment upon adjacent land owners, not necessary because more convenient ways existed, or in view of impending or intended development of the ground concerned. Rights of way might be transferred to the pavements of new streets, as was Bagley's

Stile which ran from opposite Barnes Pond to Walnut Tree Farm.

The inviolate rights of way in Barnes are shown in the definitive map prepared by the London Borough of Richmond upon Thames, dated 1981, subject to any amendments. These include the paths on Barnes Common and the Green. Certain paths to which there is access but which are not dedicated to the public have notices to that effect posted against them.

Bagley's Stile

Richard Bagley, a Barnes churchwarden through 1769–70 and 1776– 82, farmed extensive arable land in the Windmill Field north of the village and east of the river. It was served by a cartway or worple way between relict mediaeval strips loosely along the east side of Lowther Road as far as Suffolk Road. Bagley's farmhouse was opposite Barnes Pond, with the entrance to the cartway on its western side. In the usual way Bagley's name was attached to the cartway. Any earlier name is lost as is also the position of the stile. John Biggs took over from Bagley by 1791 and converted the land to market gardens, but Bagley's Stile was so known until the development of the Lowther estate.

In July 1879, Professor Henry Attwell of Nassau House, site now of 31–37 Church Road, in which he conducted a boys' school, succeeded in stopping up the part of Bagley's Stile at the rear of his premises. The magistrates condemned it as 'an old footpath between high brick walls with angles and corners which afford loitering and hiding places for disorderly persons'. The rest of Bagley's Stile remained as an earthen path varying in width between five and eight feet, providing a quiet rural walk through the market gardens and orchards to Walnut Tree Farm for the next twenty-five years. On the way it was joined by a footpath coming from Ferry Road and at its northern end bore east also to Ferry Road.

Nassau Road, taking its name from Professor Attwell's house, cut across Bagley's Stile in 1903 and three years later the magistrates consented to the stopping up and diversion of its path where it passed between 9 and 11. The certificate was granted in February 1906 'on behalf of Barnes Urban District Council and His Excellency Gerard Augustus Lowther, C.B., of the British Legation Tangier, Envoy Extraordinary and Minister Plenipotentiary to the Court of Morocco', the owner of the land.

The rest of Bagley's Stile, a little under a quarter mile, was stopped up and diverted in 1910 to make way for further estate development. The applicants were again the Council and Sir Gerard, now described as 'K.C.M.G., C.B., of the British Embassy Constantinople'. Two magistrates, John Whitcombe and Ebenezer Cobb Morley, viewed the footpath and agreed that it could be 'diverted and stopped up so as to make the same more commodious to the public and its substitution by a new highway'. This was Lowther Road. Gerard Road was made in the same year. The effect of the diversions is that the right of way in Bagley's Stile continues in the pavement of Nassau Road between 19 and 43, and in the pavement of Lowther Road on its eastern side to Suffolk Road. Walnut Tree Farm was swept away by Suffolk Road c1920.

Barnes Bridge Footway

The footway across the Thames on the downstream side of the Barnes railway bridge was opened in 1895 on the widening of the bridge and the construction of the bowstring girders. It is gained by the steps leading up from The Terrace, where there is a metal notice:

> Highways Act 1980. The British Railways Board hereby give Notice that this way is not dedicated to the public.

On the Middlesex side the footway joins Barnes Passage which runs alongside the railway embankment and then the level track for three quarters of a mile to Chiswick station. Under the provisions of the South Western Railway Act 1893 the footway is closed during the Oxford and Cambridge boat race.

Berkeley Road – Ferry Road Footpath

The hidden footpath between Ferry Road and Berkeley Road provides a patch of rurality with gates at both ends which are closed on Christmas Day and a few old trees. A noticeboard at each end states:

> Barnes Workhouse Trust. This is not a public right of way but the Trustees have no objection to the public using it until further notice and at their own risk, except on Christmas Day when both gates will be padlocked.

It is a gravel path with the brick garden wall of Westmoreland Road on the south side and a privet hedge on the north which gives way to a small squarish plot next to the grounds of the old Lowther Lawn Tennis & Croquet Club. Before development the footpath was part of a short cut to Barnes village through orchards and market gardens and into Bagley's Stile. The way is represented by the cul-de-sac end of Berkeley Road and the back garden walls between Cumberland Road and Westmoreland Road.

The Chicken Run

This is the established nickname for the footpath running from the forecourt of Barnes railway station between the upline platform and Barnes Common towards the Queens Ride overbridge. It arose as a jocular reference to the fancied impression of a poultry run with iron stanchions extending from the platform railings overhead to the tall brick retaining wall on the other side of the footpath. Near the entrance there is a metal notice which reads:

> Highways Act 1980. The British Railways Board hereby give notice that this way is not dedicated to the Public.

The footpath is entered through a brick tunnel with a barrel vault under the Rocks Lane overbridge. At the east end of the station curtilage there was formerly an iron kissing gate of whimsical design, removed after the last war. The gate swung in an openwork cylindrical structure of iron rods. The way continues with open views across Barnes Common, passing ground known to footballers as The Cressy from the house of that name in Queens Ride. The

25

footpath turns along the Queens Ride embankment to the junction of Common Road and St. Mary's Grove.

Church Walk

This pathway runs along the back entrance of the shops facing Church Road joining the southern ends of Kitson and Grange Roads. Until c1910 a Georgian house, Frog Hall, stood at the west end of the passage facing the pond with the garden running back between Church Road and this pathway. The owner of this house in 1780 was John Salter and from 1786 until 1789 it was let to George Dance, the younger, son of the architect who was busily engaged in developing the Finsbury Estate in the City. A John Salter was an artificer working on this project and there might well be a connection with Frog Hall. The Rev. Christopher Wilson, Rector of Barnes at this date, was also friendly with the Dances and invested money in the Finsbury Development even to the extent of having two streets named after him, i.e. Christopher Street and Wilson Street E.C.1.

This passage also gives access to The Grange and as a curate of St. Mary's Church was living there from 1833 to 1840 he must have found this short cut a useful approach at service times. In 1851 the Rate Book gives the address of The Grange as 'leading to the Church'. This path is clearly defined on all early maps as is also the short entrance into it opposite the north end of Glebe Road.

Cowley's Walk

Abraham Cowley the poet (1618–1667) lived at Barn Elms from retirement in 1662 until removal to Chertsey in the Great Plague year of 1665. The phrase 'life is an incurable disease' came from his pen. Cowley's Walk was loosely applied to a pleasant stretch of elms and meadow from the southern end of Barn Elms House down to the bulbous head of the vanished Long Canal adjacent to the Beverley Brook. Here Cowley would presumably take the air and ponder his writings. The name was current in the nineteenth century. Cowley's Walk is covered by playing fields. It runs along the eastern side of The Wilderness, the dense coppice on the site of Barn Elms House.

Long Walk (Barn Elms)

The lost name for the scarcely known footpath picking its rough earthen and grassy way for half a mile westwards from the towing path between the Beverley Brook and the Barn Elms playing fields to which it gives access. Stout footwear is recommended for its exploration. The path took its name from the vanished Long Canal which ran parallel with the Beverley, serving as a causeway between the two. It is entered on the Barnes side of the bridge at the Beverley outfall, passing the basin and the quiet lagoon into which the brook expands.

The path of varying width is screened from the Beverley by dense thickets of wild bushes, stinging nettles and brambles full of blackberries in due season, but with occasional glimpses of Horne Way and Putney Lower Common on the opposite bank. To the north there is a fine and continuously open prospect across the playing fields of Barn Elms, a beautifully kept expanse of bright green turf with occasional darker clumps of tall trees stretching to the horizon. The impression is of wide open country far away from Barnes. There is a private gate for Barn Elms.

There are two flat concrete bridges taking the path across the Beverley, both to Putney Lower Common, the last along the path also coming out near Barnes Common. At the western end the brookside path expands into a narrow field of coarse grass.

Long Walk (Westfields)

The name is descriptive. It is 894 feet in length, running from The Terrace on the west side of Barnes Bridge, between a high brick wall and the railway embankment to Archway Street. In the summer the embankment side is adorned with masses of white cow parsley and elderberry blossom, whilst tall chestnuts and sycamores shade the path at each end. Malthouse Passage, then called Back Lane, ran into Long Walk and when the embankment was constructed a tunnel was made to accommodate it. When Barnes Bridge station was built the tunnel was converted into a subway and Malthouse Passage was diverted into The Terrace (see Malthouse Passage).

The present Long Walk is the diversion of an ancient path into the West Field, shown in the Rocque map of 1746 crossing ploughed land to another path, now Railway Side. The original path began at the same point on The Terrace but diverged to strike Thorne Passage some thirty yards to the west of the present Long Walk. It was stopped up in 1867 at the request of James Hedgman of Elm Bank House, now the site of Elm Bank Mansions. Two inspecting magistrates found it only 5ft. 7ins. at its widest point and it was

> enclosed on either side for a portion by high brick walls, difficult to keep free of filth, the resort of idle and disorderly persons, and the land has recently changed from market ground to building ground.

The old path was stopped up. The present Long Walk was opened on 25 July 1867, when it was described as

> well gravelled and drained with a free current of air and open to the sun and light along its whole length, and /it will/ be able to be much more effectively watched and protected.

The land traversed by the old path was in 1867 marked for a new street, but it was not built over until 1896 when Elm Bank Gardens was developed.

Also in 1867 and again at the request of James Hedgman another footpath running through his estate was stopped up. It left Thorne Passage at the end of Cross Street and went on a straight north-westerly course to join the old path noticed above. The garden wall between Elm Bank Gardens and St. Michael's vicarage runs exactly along its line. Without name it was four feet wide and

> merely a trodden path, almost impassable after rain and by reason of the long grass and thorns which grow on either side of it.

The footpath was stopped up on 4 February 1867 and diverted into

a new street planned and laid out by the British Land Company Limited, called, or intended to be called, Cross Street and Archway Street.

Whilst Long Walk ends at Archway Street the route then bears past Brunel Court as a broad unnamed way and into Railway Side, following the course of the vanished embankment of the Barnes Curve.

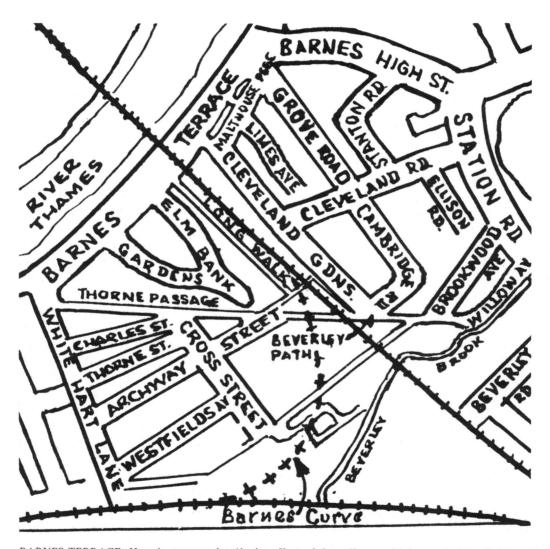

BARNES TERRACE: Here in greater detail, the effect of the railway which cut the Westfields area off from the village centre can be easily traced. In addition several of the remaining footpaths are clearly marked and the direct route of Thorne Passage shows its former importance from the riverside to the Common.

Malthouse Passage and the Back of The Terrace

Malthouse Passage is a narrow path of abiding charm behind The Terrace. Lined on one side by a row of Victorian cottages with little front gardens, it runs between the side of Barnes Bridge station and Cleveland Gardens. Before the making of Terrace Gardens the passage continued with the same name and varying width to the High Street. The old name for the entire was Back Lane, which parted the houses newly arising on The Terrace from the open outlook across the West Field. The title of Malthouse Passage, in use by the 1890s, came from the malthouse on The Terrace and other malting connections.

The development of Back Lane began slowly in the early nineteenth century until by the middle years it was crowded with cottages, stables and sheds all along the southern edge with a veritable warren of courts and alleys at the High Street end, the whole being airily dismissed as 'the back of The Terrace' or 'the back lanes'. During the last century a small colony of tobacco pipe makers flourished in the lane.

The complicated rookery of a little over two acres at the High Street end was doomed under a clearance scheme of 1911. Venturing into this quarter from the High Street the visitor encountered Morwenha Cottages, Quick's Cottages, Waring's Cottages, Wentworth Cottages, Thorne Cottages, Malthouse Cottages, Vine Cottages, Parker's Row, Long Row and St. John's Row, some within handshaking reach across the narrow alleyways dividing them. Malthouse Cottages were a conversion of an old malthouse, site now about Nos. 1 to 10 Carmichael Court flats. Over a long period it belonged to members of the Waring family, sometime owners of the Sun Inn, the Coach & Horses, the Bull's Head and a small brewery in the High Street. The last maltster was Daniel Light of Ham.

Demolition in the warren was in stages so that the 141 inhabitants could move into the new council houses as they were completed. To avoid hardship tenants were allowed to continue their old rents of from five to eleven shillings a week. Malthouse Passage at that point was widened into the present road over Morwenha, Waring's and Thorne Cottages and Parker's Row. It was named Terrace Gardens in June 1914. The first council houses were ready that summer and the second lot in September 1915, at an estimated cost of £16,800. Limes Avenue was laid out over Mr. Burree's garden grounds and greenhouses. Grove Road was extended to Terrace Gardens, with the site of Long Row, fourteen cottages, on its western side.

The relict portion of Malthouse Passage is now the north-western sidewalk of Terrace Gardens. The noticeable width of the roadway here is due to a council byelaw which required all new streets to be at least forty feet across. From the top of a bus there is a fleeting glimpse of a long room of chapel likeness with white traceried windows at the back of No. 3 The Terrace. Walking from the High Street end a pair of the first council houses stand where Quick's Cottages were at the corner of St. John's Grove. Nos. 20 to 24 Terrace Gardens and the roadway in front is roughly the site of a malthouse, occupied by a Mr. Lewis in 1783.

The narrow opening from The Terrace known from c1850 as St. John's Grove, appears in eighteenth century maps. It was sometime called 'the passage leading to the Terrace' or Wentworth Row from cottages on its western side. The origin of the present name is not known, although there was a St. John's Row in the Back Lane warren. In 1841 James Winter, a tobacco pipe maker, and his wife Sophia, a tobacco pipe trimmer, lived here. By 1861, when Mrs. Winter had gone deaf, the address was No. 2 St. John's Grove. Both may have worked for John Cook across the way in Back Lane. From the street can be seen the timber backs of two houses in The Terrace with black weatherboarding.

Continuing west of St. John's Grove there are two converted villas. John Cook's tobacco pipe manufactory was opposite between Limes Avenue and Cleveland Gardens, now covered by the roadway of Terrace Gardens and roughly Nos. 2 to 6. John Cook and his wife Lucy, a tobacco pipe trimmer, were established here by 1838. Mr. Cook, born at Hampton in 1795, made pipes of both the short and long variety from clay brought up the river to Barnes in barges. By 1851 he employed four men and two women. There are no known Cook marks or characteristics.

At the back of the manufactory was a yard and stables with two carts and horses for making trade deliveries as far as Epsom. The customers were mostly publicans. In public houses the price of a drink and a landlord's expectancy of further calls produced a small clay pipe and a screw of tobacco *gratis*. The Cook connection ceased in the early 1860s.

Horatio Nelson, born in the year of Trafalgar, a pipe maker, and his wife Sarah, a trimmer, were living in Back Lane in 1841. Mrs. Nelson, widowed by 1861, took in Charles Marshall, a pipe maker aged twenty-three, as a lodger. In 1871 he was still in Back Lane and Charlotte Hiscutt was a trimmer. Within five years he had moved to Railway Street (Westfields Avenue) being listed as a tobacco pipe maker.

Cleveland Gardens, the other narrow opening from The Terrace, appears on eighteenth century maps, but its old name, if any, is not known. On the east side there is a relic of the Window Tax, first imposed in 1696 and abolished in 1851, in a window bricked in to reduce the assessment on No. 10 The Terrace. On the east side is the entrance to Maltings Close and a pleasing door with an ogee arch. The path crosses Cleveland Gardens and into Malthouse Passage.

A malthouse is recorded in the West Field in 1862, location not known. Maltings Close, a fine residential development of 1981 fronting The Terrace and backing on Malthouse Passage is on the site of the malthouse which named the path. It was owned by John Moody in the late eighteenth and early nineteenth centuries. The malthouse is depicted with a wide arched central door and a characteristic cowl above the roof in Leigh's *Panorama of The Thames*, c1830. It was one of three malthouses in Back Lane.

The maltster on The Terrace c1830–1865 was Henry Downs who also had a large malting concern at Richmond. He was succeeded by Henry Walmsley and later by Hockaday & Alderson. By 1884 the malthouse was the Riverside Brewery of Todd & Company. During the cinema craze of 1910 the building was a venue for early cinematograph presentations in Barnes. A licence was granted for private showings but plans for a cinema came to naught. The place became the foundry of the Barnes Aluminium and Bronze Company. All vestiges of the old malthouse went in 1950 with the rebuilding of The Terrace front and the insertion of factory windows. On the 1968 OS it was marked as Brass Foundry. In 1981 the foundry was pulled down and Maltings Close built in its place in a style consonant with the period architecture of The Terrace.

The quiet cottages on the south side of Malthouse Passage sitting behind little gardens full of flowers and ornamented with blossoming shrubs appeared some time after 1867. Nos. 1 to 6 are Garden Cottages and Nos. 7 to 10 form the front row of Railway Cottages. Nos. 11 to 14 Railway Cottages are at the back in an unsuspected cul-de-sac. This is easily missed, being approached by the turn of Malthouse Passage along the retaining wall of Barnes Bridge station.

Back Lane continued into Long Walk and when the Loop Line was constructed the railway company was obliged to make a tunnel through the embankment to accommodate the ancient way. During the construction of Barnes Bridge station Malthouse Passage was diverted as of now into The Terrace. The eastern wall of the tunnel was built up and the tunnel was converted into a subway for the use of passengers. The diversion into The Terrace was enrolled at Quarter Sessions on 19 October 1915. Barnes Bridge station was opened on 12 March 1916. A request to change the name of Malthouse Passage to Malthouse Lane by one of the inhabitants in 1938 was refused by the Council.

May Lane

The original track from Barn Elms to the Chiswick ferry must have been well used before the building of Hammersmith Bridge. Beginning at the Red Lion, formerly The Strugglers, it followed the direct line to the river along what is now Ferry and Verdun Roads.

In 1908 houses were built at the southern end but extended no further than the junction with Suffolk Road. From then on the walk crossed farm land and was known as May Lane. Heavy scent from a line of these bushes pervaded the atmosphere when they were in flower, and later in the year provided winter food for flocks of birds.

After the First World War the land on the east side of the lane came into the hands of developers, more houses were built, and the name Ferry Road continued to the junction with Ullswater Road: then the London County Council acquired Bessant's Farm and the Castelnau Estate quickly came into being. May Lane lost its bushes and was renamed Verdun Road. Harrods Sports Club now occupies much of the land on the west side of Verdun Road, a reminder of the open space of the former Windmill Field.

Queen Elizabeth Walk

A pleasant walk of a little over half a mile between the Barn Elms reservoirs and the Barn Elms sports centre and playing fields. A capital place for taking the air, it runs from Rocks Lane by the Red Lion Hotel to the river and the towing path with verdant prospects all the way. The walk was first suggested by the old Barnes Borough Council to commemorate the coronation of Her Majesty Queen Elizabeth II in 1953, but because of protracted negotiations with the Surrey and London county authorities it was not made and opened until 1972 at a cost of £6,000. The land on both sides has interesting and historical associations. In this study the itinerary is described under two heads.

The northern side from Rocks Lane: Queen Elizabeth Walk begins as the sidewalk to the road leading from Rocks Lane to the Barn Elms sports centre. The Red Lion Hotel is at the corner. James Singer took over 'the Red Lyon premises and a stable' in 1718. It appears with its swinging sign in Chatelain's print of c1750. The hotel was built by 1836 after a fire the previous year destroyed the old tavern, nicknamed The Strugglers, but there is some doubt as to the continuity of the licence. In a plan of 1826 the site is occupied by Bromage Cottage (Mr. Bromage's) which appears to survive in part. Leaving the hotel and its gardens the walk passes two Boy Scout huts and the Shene Club.

The walk assumes its characteristic character on this side with the tall grassy banks of the reservoirs of 1897 which go all along to the riverside. Reminiscent of sea walls the banks often present lines of water fowl resting along the tops against the skyline. The first reservoir on the walk covers the Hop Field of eighteen acres, occupied until 1748 by James Singer of the Red Lion. There were four hop kilns or oasthouses by the walk.

At the eastern boundary of the Hop Field the road from Rocks Lane diverges through a gate, continuing privately to the Barn Elms sports centre, whilst Queen Elizabeth Walk pursues its straight course. At this point there is a gate, locked half an hour before sunset throughout the year as is also the gate at the riverside end. From here the walk runs between neatly mown grass verges and open link chain fencing.

The second reservoir encountered occupies at its western end the site of the Little Home Field, but the greater portion swallowed up Barn Elms Farm, part of the Barn Elms estate purchased by the Hammersmith Bridge Company. The Bridge Company offered the farm for sale by auction in July 1825 as the dwelling house, barns, stables, cowhouse and eleven fields laid to sainfoin, meadow, wheat, barley, oats and tares. The fields were named as:

Barn Field, Horse Leaze, Mill Meadow, Great Home Field, Middle Home Field, West Home Field, Little Home Field, the Hop Field, Shepherd's Close, Carter's Close and Great Lord's Close.

William Cobbett (1762–1835), celebrated for his *Rural Rides*, leased the farm from the Bridge Company from 1828 until 1830. The farmhouse with a range of outbuildings on each side of its yard stood well back from Queen Elizabeth Walk from which it was approached by a narrow lane. To help the unemployed Cobbett invited any who sought hard honest toil to work on the farm and in its surrounding fields. The wages each day were two pounds of bread, two pounds of meat and half a pound of cheese, with approval to sell any surplus to needs. Work began at daylight and finished at sunset.

Cobbett experimented with maize or Indian corn raised from seeds he had brought back from America, hoping to persuade people to use it instead of potatoes, but without success. He and his wife lived in the farmhouse 'close to a marshy meadow, which, I was told, would give us all agues and typhus fevers', but here are his thoughts written when at Horncastle, Lincolnshire, in April 1830:

> At this moment, five o'clock in the morning, the groves at Barn-Elm are echoing with the thousands upon thousands of birds. The thrush begins a little before it is light, next the blackbird, next the larks begin to rise, all the rest begin the moment the sun gives the signal.

After Cobbett, Barn Elms Farm was taken by the Sharp family who went in for dairy farming. On an August evening in 1889, when it was called Trowell's Farm after the occupier at that date, a great fire devoured a large barn holding the harvest of wheat and oats, a haystack and some outbuildings. The flames lit up the sky for miles around, whilst firemen took water from the lake in Barn Elms. The last occupants were the Lobjoits before all was submerged by the reservoirs.

Queen Elizabeth Walk on quitting the reservoirs crosses the hump of the flood defence wall and comes out on the towing path a little above a mile from Putney Bridge.

The southern side from Rocks Lane: From the walk there are fine open views of Barn Elms with beautifully kept turf and lines of trees against the far horizon. On the corner of the Rocks Lane entrance is the Victorian gate lodge of the old Ranelagh Club which occupied Barn Elms from 1884 to 1939. The road going alongside to the sports centre was once known as Barn Elms Lane. It passes along the edge of the airy expanse of playing fields which stretch a quarter mile to the Beverley Brook. These contain the mediaeval Great Long Croft. Here in Ranelagh days were a golf course, polo ground, tennis courts and croquet ground, taken in the last war for allotments.

Before the road diverges from Queen Elizabeth Walk to the sports centre, the water fished by the Barnes & Mortlake Angling Club is glimpsed within a coppice of tall trees. It is a small remnant of the quarter mile long Barn Elms lake, filled in 1956 onwards. The official address of the houses beyond the private gate is Queen Elizabeth Walk SW13 0DG. Next come two buildings at the far end of which rears the celebrated giant plane tree reckoned about three centuries old. It has a girth of twenty-seven feet at ground level, chains support some limbs and there is a lightning conductor. There is a glimpse of The Wilderness, a dense spinney on the site of Barn Elms, and from it runs an avenue planted with lime trees to replace the venerable elms which succumbed to disease.

Queen Elizabeth Walk running past the sports centre is screened in part from buildings by vigorous and closely set lines of conifers and ends at the towing path as described above.

St. Ann's Passage

Also known as St. Ann's Passages. The nameplates are in both the singular and plural form. It is rightangular with a long and short arm running between Westfields Avenue and Railway Side into Cross Street. The entrance from Westfields Avenue, called Railway Street until 1960, is easily missed since it runs beneath the first floor of Nos. 34 and 36. It comes out in Cross Street on the north side of the Rose of Denmark.

The passage is named for St. Ann's Cottages to which it led, a row of twenty-one small dwellings with narrow frontages and no rear access ways. The first ten were standing by 1865 and when completed three years later there was an open view across the market gardens to Thorne Passage. To fill all available space the cottages were crammed against the back of Railway Side, served by one water pump. Some ceilings were as low as 7ft. 1in. The front doors opened directly into the living rooms and coal was stored under the stairs. The cottages were condemned in 1935, together with the nearby Spring Cottages, and pulled down in 1938 when most of the ninety-nine residents moved to Chertsey Court, Mortlake, opened that year.

The reason for the alternative name, which suggests an interesting multiplicity of alleyways, is that until 1902 the passage continued on the east side of Cross Street to give access to Hinton's Row, twelve small cottages of 1865 with one water pump. The row was condemned because it was 'so dangerous and injurious to health as to be unfit for habitation'. The site was taken by the Barnes infants' school in 1903.

The passages were adorned by three public houses, the Duke of Cornwall at the entrance to Hinton's Row, and one at each end of the western section, namely the Builders Arms, now a private residence, and the existing Rose of Denmark. Going from the Cross Street end there is a broad tarred alleyway running past the site of St. Ann's Passages, now gardens with bean rows, tomato plants and a few flowers. At the western end it turns sharply by the defunct Builders Arms into a narrow path and out into Westfields Avenue.

Sprigg's Passage

This short path gives easy access from the High Street by way of St. Ann's Road to the waterside coming out between Nos. 341 and 343 Lonsdale Road. It appears unnamed on the Rocque map of 1746 and the name has now lapsed but it recalls Nathan Sprigg who built St. Ann's c1760. He was a wealthy merchant with trading interests in Jamaica. After the death of his widow in 1824, aged ninety-two, the house was willed to Miss Margaret Hibbert. Part of the garden was separated from the main dwelling by this old right of way and Miss Hibbert sought permission from the Vestry to close it on account of the inconvenience it caused to her property. The Vestry asked a sum of £500 but she obviously thought this an excessive price and the matter was dropped. This passage continues in use today and remains one of the original Barnes short cuts.

Thorne Passage and Beverley Path

Thorne Passage follows a track through Westfields which was trodden into existence hundreds of years ago by those possibly needing a direct route from Kew or Mortlake to Putney. Thus it appears to have become established as an undisputed right of way. The earliest known map of Barnes, of any reliability and detail, was made by James Taylor in 1783 and is now in the Guildhall Library. It shows the footpath running due south-east, as it does today, commencing at the junction of White Hart Lane and The Terrace. It still remains the quickest and most direct way of walking from Mortlake to Putney. The track ignored all crops and bounds in its path across individual holdings in the open field system so that those whose land it traversed were forbidden to sow or plough upon it. The footpath was always inviolate. This also applied between harvest and sowing when the cattle were let in and even centuries later to the market gardeners.

Beginning at the White Hart Lane end of the passage, where it is overhung by trees growing in the long back gardens of The Terrace houses, there is soon encountered what must surely be the oldest stretch of brick wall in Westfields. This is part of the boundary wall of the grounds of Westfields House originally enclosing a triangular piece of land upon which Charles Street now stands. The main portion was once called the Shoulder of Mutton Piece from its shape. At the apex, by Cross Street, it was known as the Little Ground, both names being current in the seventeenth century. In 1690 Thomas and Mary Penn became tenants of both pieces of land there together with a dwelling. In 1838 this was Westfields House with Owen Flintoff in residence, succeeded by Henry Coward in 1842, William Cross in 1843 and Marmaduke Hornidge in 1848.

It was Benjamin Thorne, a brewer, who had a small brewery next to the Bull's Head on The Terrace and moved into Westfields House in 1852, who gave the name to Thorne Passage, Thorne Street and Thorne Terrace in White Hart Lane. He supplied the Edinburgh Castle public house at the corner of Archway Street with his Thorne's Grey Horse brand of ales, beer and stout. The stables, coach house and stable yard belonging to Westfields House stand at the White Hart Lane end of the passage. Part of the house survives as the light engineering premises between Charles Street and Thorne Passage. Its first commercial use was as the Lily Laundry and later it became a film making workshop. Originally the grounds had been neatly laid out with flower beds and pathways while a line of trees screened the dwelling from the market gardens beyond.

Leaving Westfields House the footpath passes Cross Street, with St. Michael's and All Angels church on the left. Then a few steps further on there comes into view an unexpected picturesque spot, The Triangle. The passage then reaches the railway and when the line was opened in 1849 it had been necessary to build an embankment as an approach to the crossing of Barnes Bridge. Westfields was then decisively cut in two from north to south and an erroneous tradition grew up that Westfields 'ends at the railway'. When the Barnes Curve was constructed in 1862 there was a further curtailment of the land but provision had to be made for Thorne Passage to proceed on its way

East end of Railway Side in 1974 with the wall of the now demolished Beverley Works on the right and the overgrown plot of Gooselands on the left, This ground remains in a wild, neglected state, a curious survival from past ages.

subject to a slight deviation, thus there are two arches at this point. Despite several attempts to widen the archways into a road for vehicles to pass under the railway nothing was accomplished. In 1895 the arches were described as 'a disgrace to civilisation and ought to be done away with'. They were cited as the cause of 'much of the social lukewarmness which exists in Barnes due to the difficulty of communication' between Westfields and Barnes village.

It is here, where the footpath enters the first arch, that Thorne Passage becomes Beverley Path and on the other side of the railway the ancient way soon returns to its old route and passes more pleasant little cottages on its way across the great West Field. It is where Beverley Path meets Railway Side that there is a return to past centuries. The ground between Beverley path, Railway Side and Beverley Brook is identified as far back as 1464 as the Geseland. This was the damp meadow washed by 'the Creke' and is probably just what the name implies, a place for keeping geese. Eggs from these birds were a welcome addition to the mediaeval diet and where in villages a large flock was kept a gooseherd was appointed to tend it. Over the centuries the geseland of Barnes became known as Goslands or Goslings and Westfield folk used that term in the late nineteenth century.

In the Barnes archives the position of Goslings is fixed by reference to the lands which abutted it. On the south-west was Kirks Close and other boundaries were the Moat Garden and Liquorish Close. This latter name provides a pointer to another bygone crop. Licorice prospers on rich damp ground such as that

36

which lay by Beverley Brook. It is ready for harvesting in three years.

The entrance to Goslings, and forming part of it, was a narrow neck of land. This is now the roadway in Willow Avenue and it is into this that the footpath turns, as it does in the 1783 map, to reach Station Road which, together with the High Street, forms the north-east boundary of Westfields. The Moat Garden was between Goslings and Station Road, a site roughly occupied by the houses and gardens in the half of Brookwood and Willow Avenues butting onto Station Road. It was so named because there was a water filled moat fed from Beverley Brook which appears in Taylor's map and shows in the grounds of Grove Cottage. In 1872 the Moat Garden, alias the Moat Land, was sold to John Cowland by the Lords of the Manor for the sum of £74.15s. Its hedges had been replaced by a fence and the grounds laid out as ornamental gardens with pathways but no trace of the moat remained.

Here the old track ceases as a closely defined footpath but the walker would have been able to continue through a watersplash or, after 1792, over Creek Bridge. As flooding often occurred here, even in this century, there was no guarantee of dry feet. Then followed freedom to walk across the Common, skirting Mill Hill and on to the Common Gate into the parish of Putney.

The Tow Path

Walking down stream, the Barnes Tow Path begins at White Hart Alley and, having followed the great bend in the Thames, ends a little over three miles away at the bridge across the Beverley Brook outfall. As the crow flies the distance between these two points is only a mile and a half. An approximate line in mid-stream forms the boundary between the Surrey and Middlesex shores.

Until the turn of the century there was a floating jetty in front of the White Hart Hotel. From here, during the summer months, steamboats could be boarded for London or Richmond and it is recorded that in 1840 a trip to Margate was possible. Passing down stream the Beverley Brook relief culvert appears at the end of Elm Bank Gardens East before the walk continues under the railway bridge. Along The Terrace the towpath is now raised well above the road level as a preventative against flooding. It was quite a common event until recently for the houses opposite the river to have been inundated on the ground floor and the majority of residents kept sandbags or boards, which slotted into their gate posts, to prevent this disaster.

Along this stretch of Barnes Terrace, at the turn of the nineteenth century, there flourished a row of elm trees which were a much appreciated feature by the inhabitants of the locality. In December 1836 considerable concern was expressed about 'the cutting down and removal of the ancient trees from Barnes Terrace'. At the request of the residents the Vestry was convened and wholeheartedly supported them as presumably the order to fell the trees had been carried out by the Surveyor of the Highways without previous notification being given. So strong was the feeling of indignation that the Vestry resolved to communicate with the Lords of the Manor asking them to allow 'the expenses

The Riverside at Barn Elms 1785 by Edward Edwards and Exhibited in the Royal Academy that year. This was the place where Samuel Pepys picniced and the Lord Mayor of London feasted. The bridge over Beverley Creek can be seen in the background.

attending this matter to fall upon those who have committed the Act'. It was also agreed to send a copy to the Magistrates at Wandsworth requesting them to inform the Barnes Vestry Clerk if the Surveyor of the Highway should make any similar applications in the future. It could well have been that the Surveyor realised the trees were a danger to passers-by but he had obviously dealt with the matter in a high-handed way. Presumably new trees were planted as later illustrations show a row of young elms along the foreshore.

At the bottom of the High Street, opposite the Bull's Head, was the original position of the Town Dock. This was the chief arrival and departure place for passengers and goods using river transport and a delightful wash drawing by Rowlandson gives a charming picture of these daily events. A short distance down stream at the end of Lyric Road another landing place was later constructed which goes by the name of Small Profit Dock.

At the end of Gerard Road the riverside walk continues with an absence of traffic and considerable natural enjoyment. Wild flowers grow along the bank and tall trees along the reservoir boundary overhang the path. A variety of birds can be spotted and, especially at weekends, small river craft pass along on the water. No longer are busy little tug boats, pulling a number of barges, to be seen but the occasional Thames river steamer, bringing tourists from London to Richmond, stopping en route at Kew Bridge, adds interest to the scene. Shortly before reaching the steps which lead down to Chiswick Ferry the path widens considerably and this is the area once known as Putney Detached.

Soon after passing this ground there is a short passageway from Lonsdale

Road to the river known as Ferry Lane. Formerly there were reservoirs on either side of this entrance and a house, called Reservoir Cottage, in which the attendant lived, stood on the site of what is now the Swedish School. Noticing Chiswick Eyot on the Middlesex side the grounds and boat house of St. Paul's School are passed and Hammersmith Bridge comes into view. Here the path carries on under the bridge, past a block of flats with their private riverside gardens and the great landmark of Harrods Depository dominates the scene. This site was formerly Cowan's Soap Factory. A sugar refinery was also attached and the whole unit was named Hammersmith Bridge Works. Production started in 1858 and soon became the main source of local employment. In 1888 a disastrous fire broke out and firemen from a wide area attended the blaze, as well as floating barges, but the Sugar Works were beyond help. The fire put five hundred employees out of work. It was reopened the following year but during the bitter winter of 1890 the whole works closed down for seven weeks, causing much hardship. The Castelnau Soup Kitchen was opened up for the needy in Glentham Road but this second disaster finally brought about the permanent closure of the factory and the Works were dismantled in 1892 and many of the workers left the district, Harrods Stores then aquired the site and built the Depository which opened in 1894. Between the Soap and Sugar works lay what was known as Cowan's Field. Here for a number of years, in the late Victorian era, a Boat Race Fair was held. In 1893 it is recorded that there were 'forty seven caravans in addition to a large number inhabited by wild animals. The inhabited caravans made a population of about two hundred persons and the ground was visited during the day by many thousands of people.' All this was regarded as a local scandal and objected to by nearby inhabitants on health grounds. At length in 1894 the Fair terminated as the Barnes Inspector of Nuisances was authorised to serve notices to this effect on all concerned and the fairs subsequently ceased.

Shortly after leaving this overpowering building the grounds of Barn Elms are reached and this was a popular place in the seventeenth and eighteenth centuries for parties of ladies and gentlemen from London to row upstream and picnic. Samuel Pepys records doing so in his diary of 26 May 1667 and on several other occasions, while the Lord Mayor, and other civic dignitaries, when rowing up river in their barges frequently stopped on the sloping banks for music, dance and feast. A print of 1785 gives a delightful idea of the pleasant riverside scene. Immediately afterwards the boundary between Putney and Barnes is reached and the walker can return to the Red Lion by way of Queen Elizabeth Walk.

Trinity Church Passage

This is a broad accessway from near the northern end of Merthyr Terrace to Trinity Church Road, running along the back of the shops in Castelnau. It is named from Holy Trinity Church which stands at its southern end. The church is constructed in an early English Gothic style, aisleless, with a rose window at the west end and a turret containing one bell.

The White Hart circa 1775. Samuel Hieronymos Grimm made many sketches in the neighbourhood between 1772 and 1777. This illustration of the White Hart clearly shows the passageway to the river which formed the boundary between the parishes of Barnes and Mortlake. With acknowledgements to the British Library Board

Consecrated in May 1868 it was designed by a Lonsdale Road parishioner, Thomas Allom, on a site donated by Major Charles Lestock Boileau who, with the Hammersmith Bridge Company, also contributed to the cost of the building. Enlarged in 1913 the church lost its stained glass windows when a bomb fell on an air raid shelter nearby in 1940 causing many fatalities. The interior was rearranged in 1988.

White Hart Alley

This is the little alleyway leading down to the waterside between the Tideway Wharf flats and the White Hart public house. Steep and stoney it is part of the ancient boundary dividing Mortlake from Barnes formed by the stream which ran along the western side of White Hart Lane and the alleyway and so into the river.

Unnamed Paths and Passages

1. Until the mid 1930s a very useful short cut to Church Road was used by residents in the Rectory Road area. The passage was entered between Nos. 15 and 17 or 31 and 33 Meredyth Road and, following a line of garden fences, entered Bracken Gardens between Nos. 18 and 19. Complaints having been received by residents, whose garden fences backed onto this alley, the track was closed causing some inconvenience to all those who now had to approach transport, shops and church by a longer route via Glebe Road.

2. An old right of way ran behind Nos. 54–102 Church Road. This could be entered from the west side of Elm Grove Road and led through to Bracken Gardens. There was also access between Nos. 74 and 76 Church Road. Today the passageway has been blocked half way along and one-time stables are now converted into workshops.

3. Nineteenth and early twentieth century maps show an important farm track which crossed from one side of Castelnau to the other where the bend is positioned. It ran beside No. 122 on the south- east side and No. 125 on the north-west side. In the mid 1920s there were plans afoot to construct a major road which would bring traffic across a new Fulham bridge, divide Castelnau at this juncture and eventually connect up with the new Chertsey bypass. As the L.C.C. housing estate was also being planned the houses in Boileau Road were allotted extra long front gardens so that when the road was constructed there would be ample room to allow for its development along this route. Like so many schemes this never materialised and Boileau Road inhabitants have its failure to thank for their extra ground.

Thorne Passage between Cross Street and Archway Street. Cottages in the Triangle are to the right of the path.

5. HIGHWAYS AND EARLY TRANSPORT

The Care of the Highways

The Highway Act of 1555 laid the foundation of the law concerning highways for the following three centuries. By this act the responsibility for the maintenance of roads in each area was placed on the parish. Each parishioner, having a plough-land in tillage or keeping a plough, was required to give four days labour a year and the use of a cart to maintain the upkeep of the roads. It was possible to commute this obligation by payment or by providing a substitute; clearly this might be necessary in the case of aged or infirm residents. The act further laid down that the Surveyors, or Waywardens, should be appointed by each parish at the Easter meeting of the Vestry and as the office required that supervision for the work be entrusted to these officers on an unpaid basis it was naturally an unpopular position, although only held for the forthcoming year.

In 1691 the law was altered and the Surveyors were chosen annually by the local Justices from a list of landowners. They were obliged to survey the highways three times a year and organise labour provided by landowners or else collect payment from them. Again this was an unpaid, compulsory office, usually going round in rotation, but the work also entailed attention to the lopping of overhanging trees and shrubs and clearing ditches.

The Barnes Surveyors were dilatory in the keeping of their accounts and for the years 1744–1750 had failed to present them 'for examination and presentation' as ordered by the Justices. But this reprimand seems to have had little effect for in 1755 they were again ordered to show the reason why the accounts had not been examined or audited. No subsequent reason is given but maybe they were unaware they had neglected their duties. It must be borne in mind that at that date there were few roads in Barnes requiring such attention. It was a village off the beaten track for travellers and the footpath and bridle ways across the fields did not come under the Surveyors' orders. It might have been disadvantageous if the few roads were badly kept but, at the same time, the villagers probably felt the benefit of not being called upon to pay the Highway Rate.

In 1835 a revised Highway Act abolished statutory labour and empowered a levy of a Highway Rate, but already the Barnes Surveyors had roused themselves sufficiently to improve the High Street. In 1800 a kerbing had been laid down and in 1815 the Vestry ordered a re-kerbing with granite stone at a cost of 2s.9d. per foot. The final improvement was made thirteen years later when a drain was constructed and the cost met by compensation received from the Hammersmith Bridge Company.

By the Local Government Act of 1894 the Urban District Councils were held responsible for all roads in their parishes, other than main roads, and these latter

Castlenau at the beginning of the 20th century, looking north towards Hammersmith Bridge. The various forms of transport would cause traffic delays today.

were listed as under the care of the County Councils. At that time the chief Barnes thoroughfares consisted of Castelnau, Church Road, High Street, The Terrace, and Rocks Lane: by arrangement under the act the Barnes Council undertook their maintenance and repair in consideration of an annual payment. Until the end of the 1920s the road surface consisted of wood blocks: these were constantly in a state of repair. After heavy rain the blocks became swollen and were forced up rendering the roadway highly dangerous for both traffic and pedestrians alike.

With regard to side roads, these were affected by the Private Street Works Act 1892. Every new street was required by the Council's byelaws to be at least forty feet wide. The roadway was to be twenty-five feet in width or more and the footway on each side not less than one sixth of the entire width of the street. These conditions were strictly enforced when new roads were under construction but many earlier streets did not comply with these demands. When opportunity arose these were improved and instances of road widening occurred from time to time at the turn of the century. This was markedly so in stretches of Church Road but the High Street remains, as ever, a narrow bottleneck and a hindrance to today's traffic.

Barnes Highways Prior to the Nineteenth Century

Until Hammersmith Bridge was built in 1827 the roadways in Barnes were limited in extent. The traveller from London would most probably cross the river at Putney and then proceed along the Lower Road, pass the gate house and so

44

come within the Barnes boundary. This made Mill Hill Road an important route leading, by what is now Station Road, to the Sun Inn. Until Creek Bridge was built in 1792 it even meant fording Beverley Brook which at times flooded the roadway badly.

If the traveller wished to turn left or right at the Common crossroads a track led either to Roehampton or Richmond or else to the Red Lion and so to Church Road.

At the Sun Inn, where stood the Finger or Sign post, there was a meeting of Church Road, Common Road and High Street. This was then an important road junction and its significance was marked by the one time appearance of two inns. The earlier of the two was The Rose, now used by the Barnes Community Association, and the other sometimes referred to as the Sun Coffee House.

The highway then continued through the High Street to the river, and then proceeded along The Terrace to Coles Corner and the White Hart. At this point the parish boundary was reached and to continue further meant entering Mortlake parish.

The southern boundary of Barnes was the Upper Richmond Road but this acted chiefly as a bypass for travellers going to Richmond or beyond, bordered as it was by common land and market gardens. The peculiar shape of Barnes parish within the river bend made it an isolated and compact area for centuries until the river could be crossed at Hammersmith Bridge. It cannot be stressed too frequently how the building of the bridge and the construction of the railway altered the entire layout of Barnes from the middle of the nineteenth century onwards.

Public Transport

The earliest means of public transport whether for passengers or goods was by water. The main landing stage was at the end of the High Street opposite the Bull's Head. In 1828 a book was published entitled *The Laws and Constitution of the Master, Wardens and Commonalty of Watermen and Lightermen of the River Thames*. At the end a Table of Rates for Watermen is set out and the fare per person from London Bridge to Barnes or Mortlake was one shilling. No times are given probably as these could have depended somewhat on the state of the tide.

Ferry As its name implies, Ferry Lane, now Road, ran directly from the Red Lion to a ferry which went across to Chiswick. The wide steps which led down to the water are upstream of the pathway from Lonsdale Road to the river and the landing stage was Church Wharf by St. Nicholas Church. At one time there was a boat house for the ferry on the Barnes towpath which is listed in the 1881 census and shown on the Ordnance Survey map 1894–96. This ferry ceased to ply at the outbreak of World War II. The charge had been twopence per passenger and the last boat was named the Amie Edie.

Stage Coach Prior to the advent of the railway, stage coaches passed regularly through Barnes taking passengers to and from London. The average fare was 1s.6d. outside and 2s.6d. inside. Places could be booked and people were picked up anywhere along the road. *Lowndes London Directory* for 1798 gives a comprehensive Guide to Stage Coaches. It ran as follows:

White Hart. Strand. Daily 9am 10am noon 4pm 6pm. Sundays Winter 5pm Summer 9, 10am 3, 7pm
Bell in Bell Savage Yard. Ludgate Hill. Daily 8am 10am 3pm 6pm
New Inn. Old Bailey. Daily 8am 3pm
Spread Eagle. Strand. Daily 8am 3pm
Spotted Dog. Strand. Daily 9am 11am 3pm 5pm. Sundays 9, 10am 7pm

In 1830 there was another timetable and in addition coaches could be boarded at the Kings and Key, Fleet Street, Cross Keys, Gracechurch Street, the Goose and Gridiron and the Crown both in St. Paul's Churchyard. The service too had become more frequent and the Goose and Gridiron ran an hourly one from 9am to 8pm.

Carts Carrier carts were used by passengers travelling with goods and packages. They were less frequent as only afternoon times were given:

New Inn. Old Bailey. Daily 3pm 4pm
Pewter Platter. Gracechurch Street. 4pm
The Vine. Bishopsgate. 3pm
Kings and Key, Fleet Street. 3pm
The Silver Cross. Charing Cross. 3pm

Horse Drawn Omnibuses *The Post Office Directory* for 1870 states that the London General Company's Richmond omnibus passes through Barnes every half hour during the day calling at the White Hart and Sun Inns.

In the 1880s there was a Barnes bus which ran from the Metropolitan Station at Hammersmith Broadway to the Red Lion. The fare was sixpence and there were complaints that this was the dearest bus ride in London. The floor of this conveyance was covered with straw, there was no conductor and the driver refused to start the journey until he had looked through a small window at the back of his seat and seen each passenger drop his coin into the box provided for this purpose. Passengers sat facing each other the whole length of the bus.

When Mortlake garage first opened it was still the era of the horse and it was possible to see the small windows in the stalls from Tinder Box Alley until the garage was demolished after it ceased to be used in 1983.

Motor Transport The famous No. 9 route was motorised by 1906. The route was from Mortlake (Avondale Road) to Liverpool Street. At times, in the rush hours, this was shortened and 'Worms' were run. This was the local name given to buses which turned round at Hammersmith Broadway to bring home the passengers who alighted at the stations there. At one time No. 9s ran every three minutes and this was the second most frequent London route. Until the mid 1930s it was possible to board and alight anywhere along the route as there were no formal Request stops. Since the majority of the drivers and conductors lived in the vicinity of the garage they were well known to the regular passengers and there was much goodwill engendered among them. Other routes ran across Barnes Common via the Red Lion to Waterloo Station and Stoke Newington but the No. 9 was thought of as the local means of transport and held in particular favour with Barnes residents.

Tramways In 1901 the Tramway Company sought Parliamentary powers to make a tramway down Castelnau, Rocks Lane and across the Common to the Upper Richmond Road. The Bill was referred to a Select Committee of the House of Commons which, after hearing evidence for and against the scheme, struck out the proposal.

Among those who appeared before this Committee was the Rector, Canon Kitson, who stated that he was well acquainted with the feeling in Castelnau on this subject and he had not met with one single resident who was in favour. He also pointed out that it would be useless for the Westfields population who would be better served by a Lonsdale Road and Terrace route which would give a more direct and shorter approach to Hammersmith. Nothing further came of this matter.

Horse Power

It is often forgotten how important stabling and paddocks were at least up to World War I, and with that also went the need for blacksmiths, saddlers and cornchandlers. Large houses such as St. Ann's (Terrace), Milbourne and Essex (Station Road), The Priory, Homestead and Rectory (Church Road), to name just a few kept a horse and conveyance and coachmen are continually named in census returns. In addition, tradesmen delivered their goods by pony and trap and heavy deliveries of coal, building materials and barrels on brewers' drays required shires. The local council's dustcarts were a familiar sight with their patient creatures moving slowly from house to house and at one time undertakers' black horses, with plumes on their heads, could occasionally be seen. Stables were tucked away for these creatures in yards behind shops but the council horses were well provided for in the yard now converted into the Mortlake Tideway Development. Byfeld Gardens stables housed some of the polo ponies which came annually to play at the Ranelagh Club and their grooms slept in the lofts above. Tagg's Yard in Woodlands Road was another centre. At one time between forty and fifty horses were kept here and during the summer were used for polo at Hurlingham and Roehampton Clubs in addition to Ranelagh. Mr. Tagg also ran a riding school until 1936.

There were blacksmiths' shops beside the Sun Inn and the Watermans Arms as well as a third in Stanton Road. Mr. Duck had a saddler's shop at No. 2 High Street and corn and hay were available at Messrs. Wood & Co., 31 Barnes High Street. (Occasional Papers. No. 1. Barnes and Mortlake History Society)

Highwaymen

These colourful characters caused some dismay in the locality to travellers either crossing the Common or taking a riverside road.

The earliest recorded incidences that have been found to date mentioning Barnes took place from 1735 onwards and run as follows:

1735 – Last Thursday night about 8 o'clock, Mr. Vane of Richmond and Mr. James Bradford of the Borough of Southwark going from thence to Richmond were attacked between Wandsworth and Barnes Common by two highwaymen, supposed to be Turpin the Butcher and Rowden the Pewterer, the remaining two of Mr. Gregory's gang who robbed them of their money etc., dismounted them, made them pull off their horses' bridles, then turning them adrift, they rode off towards Roehampton, also a gentleman was robbed, it is supposed by the same two men, of a watch and about £3.4.0d. in money.

1750 – Last Friday afternoon as Mr. Gonsales, an eminent Jewish merchant, was going to Richmond in company with some gentlemen and ladies, they were attended on Barnes Common by a single highwayman, well mounted, who robbed them of their watches and considerable sums of money. Five coaches were robbed within an hour by the same man.

1771 – Tuesday night about 7 o'clock, as Edward Robinson and his servant were going to town from Richmond, they were attacked by three highwaymen on Barnes Common, who presented two pistols to their breasts while the other took from Mr. Robinson seven guineas and some silver, but did not rob the servant. They then made them dismount, cut the horses bridles, turned them adrift, and then rode off towards Mortlake.

1796.   Extract from the *Pocket Magazine*:

On Thursday evening, before dark, a fellow well mounted, armed with a brace of pistols, and a crape over his face, made three daring but unsuccessful attempts on Barnes Common to stop Mr. Peart, of the East India house, who was returning from town to Richmond. This gentleman's escape may be ascribed to the spirit and activity of the horse he was driving in a green chair, which put the highwayman himself in considerable danger, being obliged to leap his horse upon the footpath, in order to prevent his being run down, after having twice ineffectually snapt his pistol.

Col. Fullerton, of Roehampton, who passed within five minutes in his own chaise, was not so lucky. The fellow stopped him and robbed him of his purse, and a watch, valued at fifty guineas, promising at the same time to return the seals, on the Colonel's giving him a direction. He immediately after robbed a lady, of the neighbourhood, in her carriage, and two gentlemen in a hack chaise, and notwithstanding an instant alarm being given at the several gates dividing the common, by Mr. Peart, as well as the adjoining bridges, he escaped as supposed, by some of the lanes leading to Wimbledon Common.

Riverside travellers also suffered similar experiences at about the same date. Christopher Papendick, court musician to King George III, lived for a while with his wife and family on Kew Green. One evening the Papendicks were returning with friends from an 'agreeable evening's entertainment' to their home in Kew via Clapham and Barnes being driven in a coach hired from Shrubsole, a livery man at Richmond. Turning from Barnes Terrace to the beginning of 'Mortlake Lane' three men ran up from the waterside and while one went to the horses' heads the other two placed themselves on each side of the carriage and opened the door. Mr. Papendick gave them his purse, which luckily contained little money, but he was forced to alight and be searched. Nothing was found on him but a clasp knife which the miscreant opened and could not then close, so he returned it with an oath and the words, "Clear the gentlemen, we will not disturb the ladies". So saying the coach was allowed to proceed.

This misadventure did not subsequently deter Mr. and Mrs. Papendick from renting No. 7 The Terrace as their residence during the years 1807 and 1808. At that date a married daughter was living in Milbourne House so that it may well have been a wish to live near the Ooms that brought them to Barnes.

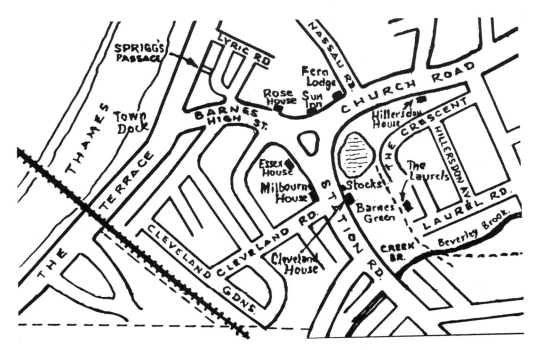

THE VILLAGE CENTRE PRIOR TO THE BUILDING OF HAMMERSMITH BRIDGE: Travellers coming from London approached Barnes via Putney and across the Common to what is now Station Road. Here stood two Inns, a Finger Post and the large houses round the Green. Church Road terminated at the entrance to Barn Elms.

6. THE COMING OF THE RAILWAYS

In spite of strong local opposition the construction of the Barnes section of the Richmond Railway began in 1845, an enabling Act of Parliament having been passed earlier that year. Construction commenced at the Putney end and moved westwards through the Common and thirteen pieces of market garden on its way to White Hart Lane and across the border into the fields of Mortlake. At the far eastern end the railway was poised to cut through the northern part of the market garden occupied by William Lobjoit between Dyers Lane annd Gipsy Lane. In September the owners, the trustees of the parish of Barnes, claimed £485.12s.6d. for the one and a quarter acres wanted by the railway, which they observed

> severs the land . . . want of accommodation in approaching the greater part for the purpose of Ploughing and Dressing the land . . . will require for protection to Fruit Land a paled fence not less than five feet in height.

In October the trustees settled for £420 and Mr. Lobjoit, whose farmhouse was in the corner of Dyers Lane and the Upper Richmond Road, received £668.11s.6d. in compensation for his loss of tenure in the ground taken by the railway.

Barnes Common was the property of the Dean and Chapter of St. Paul's Cathedral. Much scrivening ensued between the railway solicitors and St. Paul's. But in October the Barnes Commoners, copyholders of the manor, agreed to allow the railway immediate possession of ten linear acres of the Common at £200 per acre as soon as the deeds could be prepared and £2,000 invested in consols to cover the payment. Labourers with wheelbarrows descended to remove the turf as surveyors pegged the ground. The Common, in use for centuries for grazing, was almost treeless and at the end of October Mr. Knill reported that the works across it were 'proceeding satisfactorily'.

On quitting the Common the works continued westwards through market gardens between the Beverley Brook and the lane now called Vine Road. First the works clipped a small corner off William Clifford's market garden and then sliced through that of Charles Barker (Vine Road recreation ground and The Elms) who received £200. Negotiations for the next piece of market garden, which belonged to Charlotte Chapman, went on for seven months. The ground (Woodlands Road area) was occupied by Henry Higgs who accepted £215, but Mrs. Chapman in November refused an offer of £1,000 for the four and a half acres required and demanded £1,400.

In January 1846 Richmond Railway was informed that Mrs. Chapman wanted the company 'either to take the entire field belonging to her, proposed to be cut through by the railway, or build a bridge across it'. The request was not granted. In February the bid was raised to £1,350, but Mrs. Chapman steadfastly refused to sell until April 1846 when she accepted a final offer of £1,443.8s.8d., then a large sum.

The works next entered Burding Bush at the end of the journey through Barnes. Now containing the allotments next to Railway Side, it was market gardens occupied by James Priseman and in November 1845 he accepted £40 for crops and interest in the land. At this point the railway interrupted an ancient footpath which had to be diverted. This was the origin of the short and narrow length of road at the western end of Railway Side where it joins White Hart Lane.

Mr. Knill reported that several overbridges had been built between Putney and Barnes Common. Although the Richmond end had not yet started he thought the line might be completed by June, but

> if you were disposed to push there is no reason why it should not be completed earlier. The works are not heavy and delay could only arise from an inability to obtain possession of land or from a succession of bad weather.

However, in February 1846 Mr. Knill complained that he had not yet been able to get possession of land in the occupation of Mr. Cross at Barnes.

The Act called for a station to be built at the junction of the railway with the road across the Common belonging to the Hammersmith Bridge Company which it had made as part of the approach road to its suspension bridge opened in 1827. The Bridge Company had opposed the railway as 'unnecessary and uncalled for as the present means of communication between London and the districts which the line will supply are amply sufficient', having in mind its possible effect upon the tolls taken on Hammersmith Bridge.

The Richmond Railway was obliged to carry the highway, now called Rocks Lane, across the line on a bridge 'to be executed to the satisfaction of the Surveyor of the Hammersmith Bridge Company' and with a footpath on both sides. The approach embankments were not to exceed a gradient of more than one foot in thirty-five, which accounts for their unusual length. They were constructed with gravel and earth from lineside diggings. The Act further required a close wooden fence or screen at least six feet high to be erected on the parapets of the bridge and for twenty yards on each side of it

> for the prevention of damage to Passengers on such road in consequence of Horses being frightened by the Engines or Carriages travelling upon the Railway.

The engines were coke burners and threw no fire from their tall chimneys. The first bridge of one arch was rebuilt to accommodate the widening of the railway to four tracks in 1887.

There were in effect two opening days for the completed railway. The first, a year and a day from the passing of the enabling Act, was on the afternoon of Wednesday 22 July 1846. The inaugural train of sixteen carriages from Nine

Elms carrying the directors and their guests and drawn by the *Crescent* locomotive, adorned with the Royal standard, steamed through Barnes about a quarter past two, passing the incomplete Mortlake station and arriving at Richmond to the sound of the national anthem and pealing bells. On that day anyone who wished to sample the railway could apply for a free ticket to travel back and forth upon it. The opening for business was on the following Monday 27 July.

At Barnes the station agent appointed the previous month at £60 a year served the passengers, whose names were entered in a book, hence 'booking office', and issued written tickets. John Miller, the Barnes railway policeman appointed the same time at £48.8s.0d. a year had many duties around the station such as portering, operating the disc signals, locking and unlocking carriage doors, trimming the oil lamps, waving the engine drivers on and generally keeping an eye on things. In September, having discovered that the other policemen on the line were earning nineteen shillings a week (£49.8s.0d. a year) he requested that he might be paid the same, to which the directors readily agreed.

Until the tracks settled down the motion imparted to passengers was slightly unpleasant. The takings on the railway for the first week of operations were £476 and on the second £536. Villagers and children who strolled across the Common and West Fields to watch the new trains rattle past through the orchards would have seen at least two locomotives at work, the *Raven* and the *Crescent*. There was plenty of steam and shrill whistles but no smoke as engines were then required to consume their own smoke and burn coke. There was probably much hand-waving as the driver and fireman stood on an open footplate, exposed to all weathers, cabs not then being thought necessary.

The Loop Line

The Act for extending the railway from Richmond to Windsor, 'with a Loop Line through Brentford and Hounslow', was passed in June 1847. The engineer was, as before, Joseph Locke. Negotiations for land purchase were put in hand from the junction near Barnes station through a sliver of the Common and across the West Field to the river bridge and beyond. Between the lane, now Vine Road, and the Beverley Brook the line cut through the garden grounds of Henry Scarth and William Clifford. Charles Barker's orchards (Vine Road recreation ground) were now to be firmly hemmed in by the two diverging railways. On crossing the Beverley the line upon its embankment passed over market and garden grounds mostly occupied by William Burree, Thomas Parsons and Lewis Holt.

The line was opened on 22 August 1849 from Barnes, but only as far as Smallberry Green, later renamed as Isleworth station when the Loop Line reached Hounslow proper in February 1850. The new Barnes railway bridge was seen by the *Illustrated London News* as 'a light and elegant iron bridge'. It was designed by Joseph Locke and constructed by Fox, Henderson & Company under a contract with Thomas Brassey, 'the railway king'. Locke's bridge remains as the defunct upstream span of the present structure. Between 1858 and 1869 it was shared by the North London Railway whose trains traversed the Barnes Curve.

In 1891 the London and South Western Railway, having obtained powers to widen the Loop Line between Barnes and Chiswick, decided to retain the upstream span of the 1849 bridge and widen it on the downstream side. Caissons were driven to a depth of sixteen feet below the river bed, pumped dry, excavated and filled with Portland cement concrete. The new piers were capped with granite slabs and finished in yellow stock brick. The joins between the new work and the old is plainly discerned.

In January 1895 four tank engines with overall weight of 221 tons were shunted on to the new work, when it was found that the maximum deflection of the bridge at the centre of each span did not exceed 7/16ths of an inch.

Barnes Bridge station was opened on 12 March 1916, the same day that electric trains were introduced on the Loop Line. These ran half-hourly, augmented by steam trains in the rush periods. The third class fare return to Waterloo was then ninepence. Before the proliferation of private cars the station was nicknamed the Sportman's Station from the rowing and playing facilities on the Chiswick banks, reached by the footway across the bridge. The handsome entrance from The Terrace, the subway from Long Walk and the neatly tiled booking hall were all closed in 1990. Tickets are now dispensed from vending machines on the platforms. From the platforms, now gained by open stairways, there is a view of the curious side stepping of the track on the bridge from the defunct 1849 span which old photographs show crowded with spectators on Boat Race days. Tickets for this privilege were very expensive.

The Barnes Curve

The last but brief railway invasion of Westfields came with the construction of the Barnes Curve, a graceful arc of double track which left the Windsor Line one hundred yards east of the White Hart Lane level crossing. It then swung north-easterly to join the Loop Line by Long Walk. The North London Railway extended its services to Richmond and Twickenham over LSWR metals in May 1858. It gained access to the LSWR by reversing at the Old Kew Junction on the Middlesex side of the Thames, then taking the Loop Line to Barnes Junction to reverse on to the Windsor line. To obviate the tiresome reversals two curves were inserted, one at Old Kew Junction and the other at Westfields in Barnes to form a triangular junction.

In November 1858 an Act to 'make and maintain a railway wholly in the Parish of Barnes' was obtained to construct the Barnes Curve of a little over a quarter mile on a gradually rising embankment. The embankment began its rise in garden grounds of William Ratcliff and William Burree, now the allotments in front of Railway Side, from thence passing over the sites of the present infant school and Brunel Court. Other garden grounds involved were occupied by John Parks, William Burree and mainly Lewis Holt. Two tunnels took footpaths through the embankment, one for Railway Side and the other, which still exists, for Thorne Passage.

The Barnes Curve was abandoned after the line from Richmond to Broad Street opened on 1 January 1869. The embankment remained for many years as a grassy baulk lying across Westfields and limiting the eastern development of Archway Street and Railway Street. Barnes Vestry wrote to the LSWR in June 1879 asking for its removal, but a remarkable relic survives. This is the first tunnel with the curved iron ceiling at the end of Archway Street, which is presumably named for it. Grass grows on the top which carried the NLR steam locomotives and trains for seven years. The same sort of tunnel served Railway Side by the side of the present infant school. The extreme northern end of the embankment is discerned rising to meet the Loop Line adjacent to Long Walk.

Thorne Passage becomes Beverley Path when the railway crosses that former mediaeval field path. This archway supports the disused Barnes Curve built in 1858.

7. BARNES COMMON

This open ground is a great amenity for the residents providing opportunities for sports, walking and recreation. In all, the space covers approximately 120 acres but is now broken up by busy roads and railway. The majority of the paths are asphalted, but this has been done because they were formerly tracks which had been made by walkers taking short cuts across the ground to reach points of some importance, i.e. Mill Hill, the Pond, Beverley Brook and later the Railway Station.

The area from Church Road to Beverley Brook has always been known as the Green. Around this were built the large residences of the wealthier inhabitants and the names of their houses are, in some cases, perpetuated in neighbouring roads. Cleveland House stood in Station Road with its garden overlooking the Green and Pond, Hillersdon House, the Laurels, Nassau and Grove Houses have left their names to remind later generations of their former positions. Milbourne House and the much altered Essex House are the sole survivors of these villas which must have appeared of some importance to the more humble villager.

But the Green reflected a variety of aspects of village life. The Sun Inn was selling beer in 1776 when the Churchwardens' Accounts record an expenditure there in October for 1s.8d., and the Rose, now Rose House, was kept by Marjorie Gibson in 1633. The village school used two cottages in 1775 where the Day Centre is now situated and the Watch House, Stocks and Pound stood close to the Pond facing Station Road, nearly opposite Cleveland Road. In 1804 Mrs. Stanton, who owned Milbourne House, wrote to the Vestry requesting the removal of these erections from that site. The Vestry agreed to do so 'if a convenient position could be found for them'. As this was not possible the matter was dropped. In a wash drawing of the Pond by Edward Hassell in 1826 they are clearly shown on the right- hand side of the picture. Finally in 1835 these three structures were all taken down by general agreement of the Vestry and the Pound was resited by the Common crossroads. It was permissible to graze cattle on the Green and until 1830 the Town Gate was situated at the commencement of the High Street to prevent the animals wandering down it. Cows, however, were still there at a much later date.

Once Beverley Brook has been crossed the landscape alters and this area which extends to the boundary with Putney parish was originally known as the Waste. The line of demarcation between the two parishes can still be traced. The small cottage on Mill Hill Road was the Gate House, never a toll one, and a ditch was dug extending to Queen's Ride on the east and Beverley Brook on the west.

The appointment of Gate Keeper was in the hands of the Vestry and from 1777 onwards the Minutes report fully the details of those appointed to this post. In 1816 an inventory was ordered and showed details of the dwelling. This consisted of 'A Hatch Door, Bath Stove, Mantle Shelf, Cupboard with three

The earliest photograph at present known of the Gate House on the Putney–Barnes boundary. The wall of Putney Cemetery shows on the extreme right.

Shelves with Lock and Key to Do., Dresser with Drawers, 3 Shelves. Lock and Key, two Bolts and Thumb Latch to Front Door. Lock and Key with Brass Handles to Bedroom Door, a Shelf with two Brackets'. Water was obtained from a garden well.

The men or women who had charge of the gate must have lived isolated lives as they were on constant duty and in an outpost of the village but, as far as can be ascertained from the Vestry minutes, it was quite a sought after position as it provided free housing accommodation although there is never any mention of remuneration being paid. After the gate was removed the cottage became the residence of a common keeper until a pleasant bungalow was built in the garden for his use. The old gate house now has a preservation order placed on it.

Large tracts of the Waste had a sandy soil and good quality grass grew abundantly. The Churchwardens and Parish Overseers saw how profitable this could be in providing revenue for Church and Parish funds. It is recorded that in 1699 a total of 51,550 turves were sold producing £25.16s.0d. The excellence of these seem to have attained a considerable reputation and supplies are recorded as being sent far and near. In 1742 the price was two shillings a hundred, the distance of transport making no difference. Mr. Penley at Mortlake paid the same as the lawyers in the Temple. Year after year barges took turf to Scotland Yard, Fulham, Chelsea and Hungerford Stairs, to Somerset House and Peterborough House, to Mr. Kendall of Lambeth, Mr. Fleet of Bank Mill and residents of Kew and Twickenham, not forgetting 5,000 to the Prince of Wales. Mr. Tonson of Barn Elms was selective and required top spit loam at 2/- a load.

The pleasant walk across the Common to Barnes Railway Station circa 1905. The Station House, seen in the background, was recently sold to a private company and is now in use as offices.

Barnes Old Cemetery, Barnes Common 1916. Its neat appearance contrasts with its present vandalised and overgrown state. It has, however, become a sanctuary for wildlife and nature lovers.

Sand was cheaper, only 6d. a load, and delivered to Mortlake inhabitants. There is no indication that permission for this was sought from the Lords of the Manor as it should have been. In later years precise instructions had to be made on these sales as both quality and quantity were dwindling.

By 1796 the Vestry decided that further measures were needed to protect the common ground and drew up a number of rules for this purpose. These included regulations regarding the right of each parishioner to the private use of ten loads of sand annually free of expense, the refusal to allow pigs or hogs to range freely and no removal of animal dung. Each inhabitant had to pay 3d. per head per week, collected by the Common Keeper, for horses or cows turned out to graze otherwise they would be impounded. Mr. Gatwood, the keeper, appears responsible for the good maintenance of the land and also the financial side as his accounts were required to be audited twice yearly, first weeks of January and July.

In the last quarter of the eighteenth century the first encroachment was made on common land with the exception of Mill Hill. This was the erection of the Workhouse on the south side between Queen's Ride and the Upper Richmond Road; it occupied approximately four acres. However, the debt incurred to Sir Richard Hoare, the banker who lived at Barn Elms and had lent the money, necessitated the further enclosure in 1785 of about twenty acres to be let as market garden and the rent so obtained used to repay Sir Richard. This is the origin of the Barnes Workhouse Trust.

During the nineteenth century further encroachments were made on the Waste. The first in 1827 was caused by the erection of Hammersmith Bridge and the laying out of Castelnau and Rocks Lane; the latter running across the Common to the Upper Richmond Road. For these road works the Parish received £300 in compensation. Twelve years later there were further payments made when the railway was constructed and these two public works, though undoubtedly of great value, cut the Common into unfortunate divisions. Then in 1854 two acres were laid out as a new burial ground, permission having been sought and obtained from the Lords of the Manor.

Before the land was drained at the turn of the nineteenth century there were many swampy patches with mossy banks and damp hollows. It was a favourite haunt of members of the Microscopical Clubs and Natural History Societies. Even today there is a remaining swampy area off Vine Road, between the level crossing and Woodlands Road. Sixty years ago it was known as the Tadpole Pond and the willows which grew around it then remain now in forlorn condition.

Wild flowers in great profusion and in *Flora of Surrey*, compiled in 1863 by J.A. Brewer there are listed the names of thirteen rare species, some of which he describes as 'very copious' or 'abundant'. In the summer of 1907 Miss Attwell, a member of the school board, awarded a prize for the largest collection of wild flowers gathered by the girls of Westfields School from the Common and hedgerows. The winner collected 143 varieties, but the total number identified overall was 212.

Allotments became a feature during the two World Wars on the ground along Station Road to the Brook and that bounded by Cedars Road, Mill Hill Road and the Brook. A great deal of hard work was entailed by residents who were encouraged to 'dig for victory' and in many cases the crops produced were noteworthy. The only disadvantage was the danger of a bomb exploding on a plot during the night and the dismayed worker arriving the next day to find potatoes, onions and radishes scattered far and wide over a large area. Looking at this part of the Green and Common today it is difficult to realise exactly what its appearance was under cultivation. During World War I captive balloons were placed in an encampment near Mill Hill and backing onto Ranelagh Avenue. In addition there was a temporary hutment known as Searchlight Cottage which was there from 1915 to 1920. It was erected by the Admiralty and, together with the gun station on Common Road, formed part of the London anti-aircraft defences. This was originally manned by personnel of the Royal Naval Volunteer Reserve (anti-aircraft Corps) and later by the Royal Artillery. The hutment, which was used by the crew of the searchlight station, was retained for some time after the cessation of hostilities to relieve the housing shortage which existed at that time.

The Common, being part of the Manor of Barnes, by the latter part of the nineteenth century belonged to the Ecclesiastical Commissioners for England. By a scheme of the Inclosure Commissioners, dated May 1875 (confirmed by an Act of Parliament), the management was committed to a body of Conservators, one to be nominated by the Lords of the Manor and the others to be elected from time to time by the Parish Vestry. Later in 1897, again confirmed by an Act of Parliament, the management was transferred from the Conservators to the Urban

District Council. As the years passed the control moved on to the Borough of Barnes and now the Greater London Borough of Richmond-upon-Thames.

The Scheme of 1897 empowered the Urban District Council to execute works of drainage, to plant trees and shrubs for shelter or ornament and make the Common a pleasant place for exercise or recreation, but on condition that nothing should be done that might otherwise vary or alter its natural features or aspect, or interfere with free access to every part of it. The Council was further empowered to set aside any portion or portions of the Common as they might think expedient for games and to form cricket grounds. Under these powers the Recreation Ground was laid out on the east side of Rocks Lane opposite Ranelagh Avenue and football and cricket pitches have been provided. Although railings were erected around the Recreation Ground for the safety of children, no permanent fencing is allowed anywhere else on the Green or the Waste.

Gipsies

It is hardly surprising that with so much open space on common and market garden land gipsies were regularly to be found in Barnes in the last century. During the summer months they provided casual labour in the fields helping to harvest the summer crops of salad vegetables and soft fruit. Indeed they have left one clue behind them in the name Gipsy Lane and this was most likely an encampment for those who worked on the Lobjoit farm which covered that area of the neighbourhood.

Another camp site lay between the Common cemetery and the boundary of Barn Elms and when they were finally dislodged they went to live in some small wooden one-storied cottages known as Uncle Tom's Cabins. These were in Railway Side between Beverley Path and the railway arch.

Yet unknown to these nineteenth century gipsies they were supplying a source of medical information to a young doctor, Benjamin Ward Richardson, later knighted at the end of a distinguished career. He came c1845, an assistant to Dr. Robert Willis of the Homestead and before long established a good relationship with the local gipsies who did not usually avail themselves of professional medical help. His first case was to attend to a young boy whose spine had been accidentally broken by a kick from his donkey. Sadly the boy succumbed to his injuries begging Richardson not to divulge details of the accident to his parents as otherwise the animal would have to be put down. He also attended several gipsy women at confinements, all without fee, and his midwifery experiences led him to write a paper on 'The Diseases of the Child before Birth' which won him the Fothergillian prize.

For many years descendants of gipsy families lived in the Westfields area and until World War I hawked clothes pegs, bootlaces and lavender according to season around the local roads. Slowly many of them integrated with their neighbours and settled into a domestic way of life.

Barnes Common Cemetery

By the middle of the nineteenth century St. Mary's churchyard contained so many graves that it was closed for further interments by Order of Council. The result was that in May 1854 the Vestry made application to the Dean and Chapter of St. Paul's Cathedral for a grant of 'two acres from the Waste for the purpose of a New Burial Ground'. The expenses were to be defrayed by a Church Rate to be levied on the Parish. A Committee was formed and by October presented a budget for the expenditure necessitated by this project. It ran as follows:

£10 for the two acres to be paid by Church Rate. £600 for the enclosure of the ground (i.e. wall, railings and gates). £350 for laying out paths, drainage and the approach road. £50 for the Law and Consecration expenses also to be met by Church Rate. £1,000 to be borrowed at 5% from a person willing to lend this sum and be paid within ten years by annual instalments.

No mention was made of the cost incurred by the building of the chapel or the keeper's lodge, but presumably wages due to gravediggers and the keeper could be covered by funeral charges.

In 1861 a certain Mrs. Lyne Stevens of Roehampton Grove applied for permission to enclose another half acre of the Waste adjoining the cemetery as she wished to remove her late husband's remains there from Kensal Green Cemetery. She informed the Vestry she would lay out the site with trees and shrubs and 'erect a tomb of some importance to his memory'. She had even gone so far as to enlist the support of the Bishop of London who was willing to consecrate the ground.

The matter was discussed by the Vestry who approved the plan subject to the consent of the Lords of the Manor. Then nine months later the entire project was dropped and no further mention appears in the Minutes and no reason for this is recorded. It can only be presumed that the St. Paul's Dean and Chapter decided that no more Common land should be made available, or the expense proved too much for Mrs. Lyne Stevens. Finally the mausoleum was placed in the grounds of Roehampton Grove and can just be viewed by peering over the wall of Grove House which abuts Roehampton Lane.

The Cemetery served Barnes residents for the next century and also became the resting place of some distinguished Victorians whose relatives appreciated its quiet country-like atmosphere. In 1966 the Borough of Richmond acquired the cemetery and proceeded to demolish the chapel and lodge. The wall and railings which had formed the boundary were removed and sadly the whole place became desecrated by vandals. Now the damaged memorials are overgrown by brambles and many of the side paths obliterated, but wild flowers flourish giving a calming effect to an evocative area of the Common.

Mill Hill or Round Hill

Here, on the highest part of Barnes, the village mill was situated. It was common practice, in past ages, to errect windmills on commons or village greens and Barnes was no exception. Permission to do so would have been required from the Lords of the Manor, but doubtless this was not difficult to obtain as the mill helped the villagers in their meagre struggle for food and indirectly benefitted the landowner.

The earliest reference to a mill at Barnes is in the Court Rolls for 1443 which record a 'Milhyll'. The rate books from 1740-1838 mention mills and millers and from them it is possible to form some idea of its importance. Philip Walton was the miller from 1740-1761 and apparently erected – or rebuilt – a mill on his arrival and then paid rates for his house and mill which stood on land measuring 7½ rods by 6 rods. When Thomas Yewd took over from him he applied for, and apparently obtained, an extra piece of Waste 260 feet by 267 feet and continued to work the mill until his death in 1792.

During his years on the Common he was subjected to great disaster. On 15 October 1780 a most unusual hurricane struck the area. The wind swept down Roehampton Lane, across Barnes Common and so to Hammersmith causing great damage in its path which was estimated at a width of 200 yards. The mill was upturned and broken to pieces and the surrounding buildings lost their roofs. Wall, paling and young elm trees were levelled to the ground and so

This outline drawing by Edward Edwards shows the post mill overturned by the great hurricane of 1780. It is interesting to note that the date 15 October was, by an extraordinary coincidence, the same as that of the great gale in 1987. With acknowledgements to the British Library Board

This drawing by Jean-Baptiste Chatelain engraved by James Roberts in about 1750 depicts the mill on the Common looking across to the Church and Rectory. The Conduit is the small square building on the extreme right. Cattle graze freely while men are removing sand and turf which were sold by the Vestry and the money thus obtained augmented parish funds.

extraordinary was this event that a pamphlet was published concerning the phenomenon. Mr. Yewd appears to have borne this tragedy bravely for three years later the mill was rebuilt and working again but then it was a smock mill and the old post mill had gone forever.

The names of two more millers, Stephen Page and Thomas Falkner, appear in the rate books and by 1827 the last one, Charles Trock, took over the cottage and mill. He kept going until 1836 and then in the following year the entry states: 'Late Trock. Cottage, windmill, etc.' and in 1838 'Late Trock. Cottage' but there is no mention of the mill and it never appears again. Sadly the last Barnes miller died in Richmond Workhouse, presumably in an impecuniary position.

The mill site was then built over and today it is difficult to judge the original positioning. An *Atlas of London and its Environs* published by James Wyld, 1st edition 1849, names three properties there, Windmill Hill Cottage, Bell Cottage and Castle Cottage, and two years later the 1851 census returns refer to Yewds Cottage. By 1861 Windmill Hill Cottage had been shortened to Mill Hill Cottage and gradually the site has been developed over the years but the area covered has not been increased since Yewd obtained his extension in 1763.

The Smock Mill, Mill Hill, Barnes Common circa 1808. It replaced the Post Mill which was blown down in 1780.

8. HOUSING DEVELOPMENTS

Westfields

In December 1865 a mere £1,296 secured the freehold of the so- called 'Little Chelsea' area in Westfields, Barnes. It was mostly market garden ground consisting of a patchwork of fields, which had enjoyed centuries of common use and had been known as Thameshot, Le Headlands, Longlands and Middlelands. Here were built Railway Street (now Westfields Avenue) and part of Archway and Cross Streets.

Eleanor Grove went up on the southern half of Burding Bush, an eight acre field, through which the railway had come in 1846 and cut Westfields in two, and by 1880 Thorne Street and Charles Street were added. Prior to the erection of these last two streets, Railway Side from No. 20 eastwards was already standing together with Manor Cottages and St. Ann's Passage. Then the eastern limb of Archway Street was completed to the railway and Cross Street extended from the junction of Archway Street to Thorne Passage.

But not all of rural Westfields – the final 's' came in the early nineteenth century – was to disappear beneath the pavement. Those who tend the allotments and bean rows south of Railway Side are carrying on the homely tradition which brought the West Field of Barnes into existence many hundreds of years ago. Then it was a question of working and watching the land or suffering a meagre harvest.

The West Field was one of the enormous open fields of mediaeval Barnes in which a system of husbandry was practised to manorial rule. It was balanced by the North Field, another great tract, on the other side of Barnes High Street. This was called Norton Field, alias Windmill Field, later Northtown, which extended to Norton le More, or the Great More on the damp margins of today's Castelnau peninsula. The Thames was one boundary and it was served by two worple ways. These were Norton Lane (now Grange Road) and Twelve Acre Lane, later called Bagley's Stile, a part of which shows between Nos. 9 and 11 Nassau Road. But to return to Westfields, as the village population grew it was necessary to extend the arable land by cultivating more of the wastes on both sides of Barnes High Street. In Tudor times, when Westfields was probably four hundred years old, it was called Westonfield and more familiarly Weston or Westoney. Sweep away all roads, houses and railways from White Hart Lane to the back of the High Street and Station Road and from The Terrace to Beverley Brook. Replace them with arable strips and pieces, with meadows by the brook, and you have the West Field in its fully-developed form.

Open fields were divided into furlongs and there is evidence of such a layout in Thameshot (earlier Temmyshote), the furlong now occupied by The Terrace. Here the long narrow back gardens could be the fossilized remains of some of the West Field strips but the divisions in the West Field are often irregular.

The strips and pieces were allocated by lot or a similar system to give each person a fair share of good and unfavourable land. In early times the crops were presumably corn, beans, peas, barley, oats and rye. Vegetables such as onions, garlic and herbs for medicinal use and fruit were grown in the crofts attached to each homestead, or homestalls as the Barnes archives call them. If Barnes followed the customary arrangement West Field and Norton Field were worked in rotation with one of them lying fallow in turn, while between harvest and sowing the cattle would have been turned out to graze on the stubble.

There was thus inevitably a great deal of going to and fro between all parts of the system to work in the various strips. Take William Goodchild's holdings in 1517. He had a cottage and homestall of 6¼ perches and his husbandry in field and meadow took him to Temmyshote, the Short Lands and Middlelands in the West Field. He had other pieces in Norton Field and in Town Lambcroft and Lambcroft near 'The Grene' and meadow land in Moremead (now Ranelagh Avenue). The rent was ten shillings (50p) per year.

Conjuring up the West Field of the olden times and looking across the acres of flat fields the disadvantage of the open field system is obvious. To get to his own pieces and strips the Barnes villager had to cross those of his neighbours and they his. And a footpath (Thorne Passage) passed through all on its way. Individual holdings were bounded by grass baulks or rough fences and somewhere in the West Field was the Markheyge (mark hedge) which had some important function. The keeping of adequate fencing was a serious matter. It was vital to keep cattle from entering pieces under cultivation. The priest of Barnes church was fined 6s.8d. (33p) in 1433 for failing to repair 'severall ffences at Lachfurlong', and even the Lord's Under-Bailiff was in trouble for not keeping out the hogs 'by which divers men and tenants have had great damage'.

There are great gaps in the Barnes archives, so that intuition and painstaking detective work are needed to sort out the location of named places in old West Field but sometimes the field name gives its own clue. For example, Goredhawe was almost certainly gore or wedge shaped, but there are many such pieces. The hawe part of the word denotes that it was probably an enclosure. Hawthorns were then, as now, employed to give impenetrable hedges and are so named.

In other cases locations are identified beyond doubt. Pyked Acre, alias Picked Acre, was named from its long narrow pike shape. Today it is now part of the council estate at the bottom of Willow Avenue. The footpath leading from Railway Side under the railway to Beverley Path is one of the boundaries of Pyked Acre. It is found mentioned as early as 1493 in the reign of Henry VI. In 1518 John Warde worked an acre of land in it and paid 11s. (55p) for it together with his homestall and orchard. It continued under cultivation through the centuries – Burree of the well-known market garden family had it in 1783 – until its old name was half forgotten and by 1839 it was quaintly corrupted to Peter's Acre. However, it was as Piked Acre that Thomas Cubitt and Julian Roberts took it in 1862 and began to build Manor Cottages on it two years later.

Longlands, Shortlands and Middlelands, all part of the mediaeval open field system, explain themselves. There were also the Headlands the meaning of

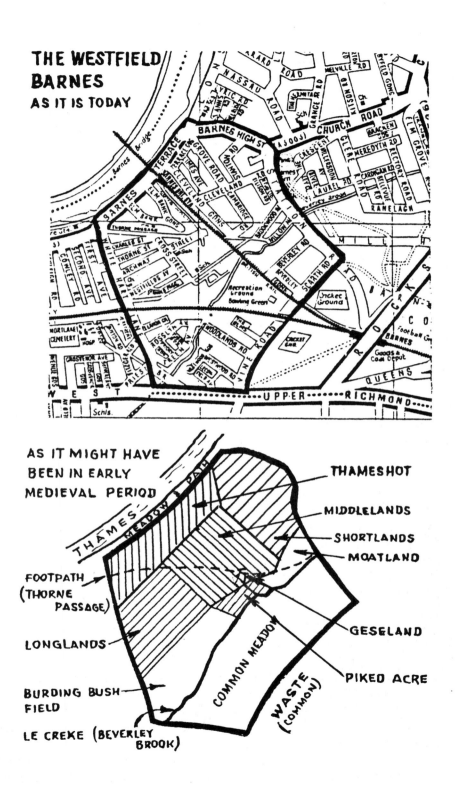

THE WESTFIELD
BARNES
AS IT IS TODAY

AS IT MIGHT HAVE
BEEN IN EARLY
MEDIEVAL PERIOD

THAMESHOT

MIDDLELANDS

SHORTLANDS

MOATLAND

FOOTPATH
(THORNE
PASSAGE)

LONGLANDS

GESELAND

BURDING BUSH
FIELD

PIKED ACRE

LE CREKE (BEVERLEY
BROOK)

COMMON MEADOW

WASTE
(COMMON)

which is the strip of land at the ends or boundaries of fields where the plough was not taken.

In 1847 consolidation of part of the West Field began when Henry Scarth of Putney Park was admitted by the Lords of the Manor of Barnes to 24 acres of land, mostly market garden, in the West Field, at customary fee. The land consisted of Thameshot, Le Head Lands, Longlands, Middlelands and Burding Bush. The previous owners of the various copyholds included members of well-known Barnes families including James Goodenough, William Roffey, James Priseman and William Misplee. Eighteen years later Henry Scarth, whose name is perpetuated in Scarth Road, came before William Sellon, steward of the manor, on 3 July 1865 and surrendered the copyhold to the British Land Company Limited for £5,700. On 10 August Walter Elliott Whittingham for the British Land Company Limited appeared before the steward 'in his own proper person . . . and prayed of the Lords of the Manor to be admitted tenant forthwith out of court to the said 24 acres'. Copyhold was granted and it only remained for Mr. Whittingham to obtain the freehold for £1,296 and go through the final manorial transaction on 30 December 1865.

The way was now open for the development of today's 'Little Chelsea'. Within two years of the sale streets were laid out and awaiting the builders who were to line them with cheap terraced cottages. The Court Roll entries of the British Land Company's transactions occupy several pages of beautifully written script, the wording conforming to the formula which had been in use for centuries. Mr. Whittingham was to 'enjoy the rights of common as he did as a tenant' before enfranchisement.

The area developed rapidly. Families quickly moved in, schools were built for infants, girls and boys, of which only one remains today. The spiritual needs of the community were of concern to the Rector of Barnes and a Mission Church was set up in 1867 being used by day as a Junior Mixed School. From this small beginning there arose a need for a larger and permanent place of worship and eventually St. Michael's Church was consecrated on 26 January 1893. At first it was a daughter church of St. Mary's, with the Rector appointing a priest in charge, until in 1919 Canon Kitson decided it should be a separate parish and appointed his nephew, the Rev. Bernard Kitson, as the first Vicar.

This 'housing estate' quickly developed a life of its own. Although White Hart Lane was its main High Street of shops yet a number soon opened to serve the more immediate needs of the residents. For some unknown reason Charles and Thorne Streets were excluded from trade but Archway, Railway and Cross Streets had a variety of goods to offer and doubtless the residents of Charles and Thorne Streets availed themselves of the opportunity to purchase requirements. There were several sweet shops, a number of small grocers, two greengrocers, bakers, butchers, fishmongers, drapers, boot repairers, corn merchant and at one time a fried fish shop. The thirst of the residents was well supplied with a number of public houses which were probably a means of escape from the overcrowded conditions of the cottages and were a form of entertainment, although on Saturday nights they were often the scenes of noisy brawls. The Manor Arms and The Rose of Denmark are still open, but most regretted is the change to a private dwelling of the Beehive at 36 Railwayside. This faced the allotments and had a truly rural aspect. The front entrance had a projecting canopy overhung with Virginia creeper which, in autumn, showed a fiery red colour, truly a delight to the eyes of all those who passed by.

To offset the attraction of the public houses The Welcome Coffee Palace was established at 54 Railway Street and opposite was the Welcome Mission Hall. Lord Radstock, of East Sheen, was the owner of these premises. He conducted evangelical and philanthropic work there and held Band of Hope meetings for the children. Later the Mission Hall was taken over by the Salvation Army.

Today's residents in their neat, tidy homes with colourful little gardens and window boxes would have difficulty in recognising this area at the turn of the century. There was then genuine poverty, children ran around raggedly dressed and in summer bare-footed to save footwear for winter use. Large families were crowded into the small houses, bathrooms unknown and unemployment a serious matter when there was no national assistance. The men's work was often affected by bad weather and the soup kitchen, run from St. Michael's Church, was greatly appreciated as were the blanket, coal and clothing clubs. In the days before school dinners there was a church fund to provide necessitous children with a hot meal and a maternity society to assist mothers. The better off Barnes residents showed real concern for their less well-to-do neighbours in those late Victorian days before the Welfare State had been envisaged. Westfields has indeed changed more than any other area in Barnes history.

Housing Estates

The building development of Barnes has been piecemeal since the middle of the last century and has occurred earlier than many London suburbs. The first reason for this expansion was the building of Hammersmith Bridge in the 1830s. This was followed by the coming of the railway twenty years later. Apart from the large houses centred round The Green, the Church and The Terrace, with the cottage property in the High Street, the land was largely devoted to market gardening so there were acres of ground 'ripe for development'.

Castelnau and Lonsdale Road These thoroughfares were first known as Upper and Lower Bridge Roads and they owe their appearance to the Hammersmith Bridge Company which was formed in 1827. Building began – albeit in a piecemeal fashion – commencing from the Bridge and slowly making progress towards the Red Lion or The Terrace. It is interesting to notice how the houses in Castelnau were built either in short terraces or pairs giving an attractive variation the length of the road. At one time, before Castelnau was completed and numbered, all houses were named and also divided into groups such as Church Terrace and Castelnau Villas. Lonsdale Road was similarly treated and the earlier buildings can easily be identified being of a much more pretentious nature than the semi-detached ones now facing St. Paul's School.

Station Road Development   From the 1850s another section of Barnes was in demand for development. Commuters were in need of housing not too distant from the railway station which was built in the centre of the Common. Consequently Scarth Road, Station Road, Cleveland and Woodlands Roads and a section of Beverley Road were sought after by the family man who was engaged in business in the City. As these properties were adjoining the Common this area was much favoured for its pleasant environment.

Glebe Lands   The Dean and Chapter of St. Paul's Cathedral were the ground landlords of large tracts of land but slowly had disposed of property leaving only Church property under their jurisdiction. At the turn of the twentieth century it was decided to allow building on much of this ground on leasehold terms and the ground rents would be used to augment the Rector's stipend. This estate included Kitson, Melville, Ellerton and Meredyth Roads, all named after Barnes Rectors, as well as Glebe and Rectory Roads. It was not until after the Second World War that residents here were allowed to purchase their freehold.

White City   Between 1912 and 1914 an interesting estate grew up on the east side of White Hart Lane close to the Upper Richmond Road. These roads which include Priory and Tudor Gardens and Treen Avenue were nicknamed The White City as their white stucco facades reminded people of the exhibition centre at Shepherd's Bush. For many years Beverley Brook formed a natural boundary to this estate and the residents were obliged to make a lengthy detour around Hogger's Corner to reach the Common and the Station. Eventually in the 1950s a footbridge was erected across the stream giving access into Woodlands Road for pedestrians.

Lowther Estate   After the First World War the housing problem became even more acute and there were still large open areas in the district. These fields were the property of the Lowther family and extended from Nassau Road along Lonsdale Road and the back of Castelnau almost to the Boileau Arms. The west end of the ground was sold to private builders and the names of the roads bear witness to many of the overseas places where members of the Lowther family had served in diplomatic positions, i.e. Washington, Madrid and Galata, or those associated with their English properties such as Cumberland, Westmoreland, Suffolk.

Castelnau Estate   By 1925 the London County Council had embarked on extensive housing schemes for their poorly accommodated residents. Having built extensively on the Putney Park grounds and at Eltham and Dagenham they were forced to look for yet a further site for the overcrowded people in Fulham. Here in Barnes, not too far off, was a sufficiently large space for over 600 houses. Accordingly land was purchased and for the next three years house building proceeded at a great rate. Families moved in piecemeal, as soon as a few houses were ready, and as every new tenant was a family man so the

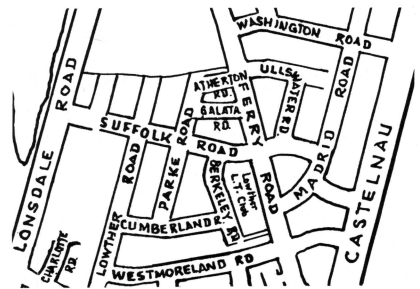

THE LOWTHER ESTATE: *Lord Lowther had acquired a large acreage of Barnes land when he purchased St Ann's in 1846. It was used as market garden ground until after World War I with the exception of Madrid and Westmoreland Roads.*

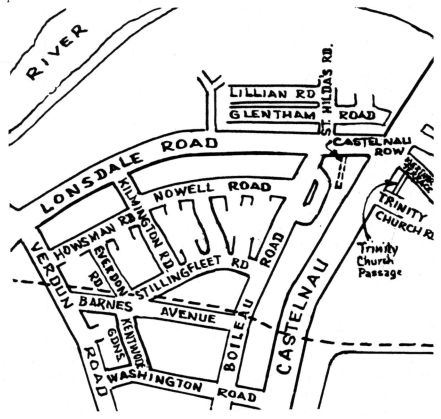

LONDON COUNTY COUNCIL CASTELNAU ESTATE: *The dotted line across this map shows the proposed road of the 1920's which would have necessitated bridge building in the Fulham area. The Barnes stretch of the road was planned to follow an old farm track which had earlier been used on the Barn Elms estate.*

71

A view from a bedroom window of a Kitson Road house in circa 1907. At that date the last house built in Melville Road was No. 35 and then from there on market gardens stretched across open land to the river.

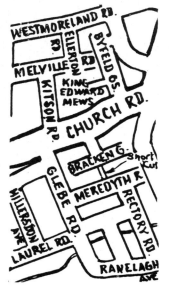

THE GLEBE LANDS: *Early in the 1900's much of the Glebe land was used for house building. No. 99 Church Road was erected on a paddock where former Rectors had grazed their horses, while the Rectory garden was very curtailed when Nos. 2–12 Kitson Road were built on the grounds formerly used by parishioners for Church Fetes and Sunday School treats.*

Castelnau Row: Then and Now. Two photographs taken about thirty years apart, showing how this enclave has altered during that period. The wall and high chimneys shown at the end of the earlier picture were those of Castlenau Place demolished when Boon and Porters Garage was extended in Castlenau.

Barnes population increased by 2,500–3,000 where only one family, living in a farm house, had resided. The names of the roads recall former Deans of St. Paul's Cathedral as they were the original ground landlords. This entire estate came into the parish of Holy Trinity and to meet the spiritual needs of this area a church hall was erected by the parishioners in Stillingfleet Road. This is now used as a Youth Centre. Owing to the size of the child population, schools were erected which, at one period, were so full that overflow classes used the Church Hall during the day. One inconvenience which was felt by the women folk was that no shop was erected but this appeared to be the general policy of the L.C.C. at that date. A strong residents' association was formed and annually prizes were awarded for the best kept front garden. There was great competition to become a prize winner.

Small Developments on the Grounds of Private Houses House building continued in this way as large houses were demolished and adds much to the variety and pleasures of the neighbourhood. In many cases the names of the roads give clues to the sites of former residences and their inhabitants. Interested readers should refer to *Street Names of Barnes, Mortlake and East Sheen* compiled by R.C. Gill LLB and published by the Barnes and Mortlake History Society.

Enclaves

It is not easy to define an enclave for undoubtedly a friendly atmosphere enters into the title, but it appears to be generally agreed that it is an enclosed area with a single entrance and exit. It cannot be assumed that all cul de sacs fit into this category for an enclave seems to demand some individuality either of houses, layout or style. Natural features contribute much to the friendliness of the area and where dwellings have been built on the site of former private property an enclave can be seen to best advantage. Grass and trees and, as in the case of Castelnau Row, no traffic add very greatly to the charm of the surroundings. Although, in some cases, enclaves are uneconomical with space, modern developers are realising that a good use of the environment is appreciated by many home buyers.

Banjos This curious title was given to the small enclaves off many of the roads on the Castelnau housing estate. The houses, in small groups, were set back from the main building line with a small communal grass area thus giving the appearance of a village green. The estate was laid out by the London County Council in the 1920s and part of the intention was to give as much open space and fresh air as possible to the newcomers. Many of the early residents spoke of 'living in the country' and certainly the design of the banjos contributed to a homely atmosphere which was greatly appreciated.

Castelnau Row, Lonsdale Road In May 1844 the Vestry agreed that the rates on the cottages in Castelnau Row should be assessed at £7 per annum each. Thus it would appear that these dwellings had been newly built and were being considered for the first time.

This charming group of seven small cottages, originally built two up and two down, now tucked away in its grassy plot, is hidden away behind houses in Lonsdale and Boileau Roads. The narrow passage leading to this enclave is named Bull Alley on the Ordnance Survey map of 1867, a seemingly strange name for such a quiet retreat.

The Elms   The Elms consists of a group of town houses tucked away behind older residences in Vine Road. Built on the one time extensive garden of Ivy Walls it can probably best be viewed by travellers on the railway line between Barnes and Mortlake stations. The narrow entrance between two houses in Vine Road is unobtrusive and could be missed by those walking or driving along the common thoroughfare.

Essex Court   This is an interesting Council development set in the former garden of Milbourne House and laid out with a central green open space. Its erection followed an eight year fight to save Milbourne House from demolition after World War II as the Borough Surveyor in 1945 considered the house had outlived its usefulness, was devoid of any charm and its age was against it. The struggle (see *Milbourne House, Barnes* published by the Barnes and Mortlake History Society) at length was resolved by a compromise. For £3,000, plus legal expenses, the owner was prepared to sell the extensive garden area to the Council on condition that Milbourne House was to be allowed to remain.

Essex Court bears the name of the two men formerly connected with the estate, for at the end of the fifteenth century a certain William Essex had acquired the property and it became known as 'Essex Place, otherwise Milbourne'. Later it became Crown property owing in 1554 to the execution of Thomas Wyatt as a traitor and Queen Elizabeth I leased it to Robert Devereux, Earl of Essex. Whether he ever used the dwelling is unknown but he, in his turn, leased it in 1592 to Robert Beale, Francis Walsingham's secretary.

The Hermitage, Grange Road   This housing development of the 1950s was carried out on land once the property of James Goodenough who paid rates for it in 1793. The property was then called Hermitage Cottage and it was here that the eccentric author of *The Monk* and *Castle Spectre*, Matthew Gregory Lewis, lived from c1801 until his death in 1818. He wrote lengthy letters to his mother describing this rural retreat and here, one summer's day, he entertained the Duchess of York and her suite to an outdoor '*dejeuner a la fourchette*', she having driven over from Oatlands. Music filled the air while the Duchess nursed his favourite tortoiseshell cat, Minnette, which she enveloped in her shawl.

By 1851 an imposing dwelling had been built facing the road with a driveway in front and large garden at the rear. It was then named Hermitage Lodge or The Hermitage and in 1861 provided accommodation for Samuel Martindale, a married barrister with a family of seven children plus an adequate staff. It continued in private ownership for many years and when the Oertling family were residents in the 1920s the well-kept garden was the scene of many a summer fete. A raised bank at the far end provided an admirable stage for outdoor concerts and amateur theatricals and it was then still possible to trace the old route of Bagley's Stile from Nassau to Gerard Roads.

Now this one time private plot has become an enclave of town houses and flats providing homes for many residents in a secluded setting.

King Edward Mews   The dwellings in these mews are converted from former stables used by polo ponies. During the summer months many players of polo arrived for the season at Ranelagh Club with their own horses and here, in Byfeld Gardens, was an opportunity to keep them close at hand. Their grooms, often Indian servants of maharajahs, lived above the stalls and it was a common sight, even as late as the 1920s, to see riders and ponies exercising at a discreet pace in the local roads during early morning hours.

Sheridan Place Sheridan Place is a recently erected group of dwellings designed for elderly residents. Approached from Brookwood Avenue, Beverley Brook is crossed by a bridge built in warm red brick with stone globes at each end of its curving parapets. The houses stand on the site of the former Beverley Works which closed in 1971. This enclave takes its name from Tom Sheridan, son of the famous playwright, who resided with his family at Milbourne House in 1810.

The Triangle, Thorne Passage   This small area is not named in maps or directories but is formed by a group of cottages in the part of Thorne Passage between Cross Street and Archway Street. The cottages concerned are Richmond Cottages and Sydney Cottages and those in Thorne Passage itself. They stand with picturesque front gardens giving a countrified effect to the passer-by. Richmond Cottages are probably named from a malthouse owner of that title.

A Corner Shop at the junction of Westfields Avenue and Cross Street in 1977.

9. UNUSUAL SITES AND BUILDINGS

Coles Corner and The White Hart

Coles Corner was the old name for the junction of The Terrace with White Hart Lane. It was known as that in 1676.

The White Hart Hotel was originally named The King's Arms but the name was changed sometime previous to 1764 so that it may be presumed that the naming of the thoroughfare dates from around that time. As this point marks the boundary between the parishes of Barnes and Mortlake it was an important position in the locality. It is from here that the ancient footpath – now Thorne Passage – begins its course across the Barnes lands.

The name Coles Corner remained until the last century.

Lammas Land

The use of Lammas Land was the immemorial right of parishioners to graze their livestock on parish land annually from Lammas Day (1 August) until sowing time.

The land in Barnes lay in the northern part of the parish and the first loss occurred in 1783 when the Windmill Field was enclosed for the annual payment of £20 and the Lammas privilege was thus taken from it.

More serious was the disruption in the next century, firstly in 1827 in connection with the building of Hammersmith Bridge and four years later in connection with the West Middlesex Water Works. This latter company required fifteen acres of meadow land for the construction of the reservoirs and, after negotiations, a settlement was agreed in 1831 that an annual rate of £1 per acre should be paid to the parish.

The final disposal of Lammas Land occurred in 1847. There was an unenclosed field, known as Sprigg's Piece, part of the St. Ann's estate, situated in Lonsdale Road where Walnut Tree Close has been built. Lord Lonsdale had purchased the house and grounds the previous year and then written to the Vestry requesting permission to enclose the field by 'paying yearly to the Parish what remuneration they may think a fair and proper compensation'. A reply came from the Vestry agreeing he might enclose Sprigg's Piece 'on condition of his paying the Rector and Churchwardens for the time being the sum of £6 per annum to be disposed of by them in Bread for the Poor and also leaving open the footway leading from Bagley's Style to the Windmill Field'. Lord Lonsdale agreed at first to these terms but ten years later the Parish gave him permission to buy these four acres and the price agreed was £798 which was invested in Consuls. This was then known as the Lammas Land Trust.

Putney Detached

Putney Detached was a piece of land about twelve acres separated from Putney parish, but counted as part of it. It lay in Barnes by the Thames, opposite Chiswick on approximately the site of the wildlife reservoir and opposite to Mill Lodge. Such detached parts of parishes were fairly common until the nineteenth century when most of the remaining ones were abolished.

One theory is that Putney Detached was the site of a fishery mentioned in the Domesday Book, 'Earl Harold established it ... on St. Paul's land'. The reference being to the Canons of St. Paul's Cathedral. But the more likely use of this land was meadow land or Lottmead. The ground would have been divided into strips and hay grown on it to help feed cattle during the winter months. The fact that a man's 'lott' was some distance from his dwelling was not a matter of great consequence as it did not require constant attention. By the 1680s two Barnes residents, Emerton and Snignall, were tenants of a large portion of Lottmead so it appears gradually to have become an ordinary group of fields or meadows, peculiar only in that rates and rent were paid on it to Putney parish.

Finally in 1906 the Barnes Urban District Council minutes record that an Act in Connection with Putney Detached obtained Royal Assent and, possibly after nine hundred years, was transferred to Barnes.

The Rose Acre

Mr. Edward Rose, a citizen of London, was buried in Barnes Churchyard in July 1653. His grave is outside the south wall to the east of the porch, the oldest one in the churchyard.

By his will of the previous year he bequeathed £5 for a wooden frame and requested that three or more rose trees should be planted about the place where he was interred. He also left £20 to the minister, churchwardens and overseers of the poor of Barnes to be invested in land upon trust to keep the frame of wood in repair, the rose trees preserved and gifts to the poor of the parish. Accordingly an acre of land was purchased in Town Long Croft adjoining an acre called Church Acre and the churchwardens' accounts illustrate that his request was carefully complied with.

In 1746 John Nightingale of Cleveland House was desirous of becoming the owner of both pieces of land and proposed to give in exchange two acres of freehold at the southwest end of Common Close. This was agreed to and he then took a lease of the said two acres of freehold at £5 per annum. By the early 1800's the rent paid by a subsequent tenant was £8 and from 1834 for a number of years £8 10s. In 1849 Mr. William Clifford took a lease of 21 years at a rental of £7 per annum undertaking to make an outlay of £130 in building a cottage on the ground. By now the area was reduced in size as the South Western Railway Company had purchased a portion. In 1870 the question of releasing came up and Clifford offered £42 per annum and to build two villas and a cottage to the value of £1,000. At first this arrangement was approved by the Vestry but was later rejected in favour of an offer by Mr. Butler Rigby who was prepared not only to pay the same annual rental but also to erect two substantial dwellings facing the Common and also not less than three pairs of cottages 'of similar character to one I occupy in Beverley Road'. These houses are the ones in

Beverley Gardens. As Clifford was an old inhabitant and tenant this decision caused much dispute at the time and was considered very hard and unfair by many of his friends.

Originally the income from Rose Acre was used to purchase bread which was distributed to the poor attending church on Sundays, Christmas Day and Good Friday. However, by 1879 the plot was sold and the money invested in Government Stock under a scheme of the Charity Commissioners for the future administration of the charity.

Small Profit Dock

It is a popular belief in Barnes that Small Profit Dock near the western end of Lonsdale Road was so called because it did not make enough money, but this is not so. It took its name from its situation in a piece of land known as Small Profit, a common enough name for unproductive land or awkward land to work, which was presumably the case with the land on this part of the waterside at Barnes. The name occurs in the Vestry Minutes of February 1828 when the Hammersmith Bridge Company sought to make a new road from the suspension bridge by way of Chapman's Farm, Goodenough's Field and Windmill Field 'to a piece of land called Small Profit'. It was to continue in front of Mrs. Margaret Hibbert's house (St. Ann's) and the brewery to join The Terrace. At that time the ancient drawing or town dock was on The Terrace near the bottom of the High Street and so John Roseblade, the Vestry clerk, was instructed to write to the Bridge Company's representative to enquire how it was to be preserved 'as the plan of this New Road gives no information on the subject and a Meeting of the Inhabitants will be called for Thursday next at 12 o'clock to take the same into consideration'.

The Hammersmith Bridge Company countered by offering to build a new dock to take the place of the old one 'and that in the event of the proposed New Line of Road to Barnes Terrace being effected that Provision will be made for a Landing Place very Superior to the present'. But opposition to the proposals grew. Mr. Hoare dissented to the new road and Mr. Biggs said he would not continue to pay the parish £20 a year for 'the privilege of inclosing Windmill Field' if it was built. Mr. Hillersdon was also against it and a deputation was appointed to wait on the Bridge Company which informed it that 'having procured the consent of the City of London to extend the proposed Line of Road into the River and to remove the present Dock from the East End of The Terrace to a piece of land called Small Profit it having been represented to them that the present Dock was a nuisance to The Terrace and that the removal of it to Small Profit would be a convenience to the Parish of Barnes but they wished to have the opinion of the Vestry . . . as they had not finally determined in Removing the Dock'. Much correspondence passed between the two parties but the new road was eventually made. Today this is Lonsdale Road. The new landing place was aslo made and as a matter of course it became known as Small Profit Dock.

Today this dock is seldom used but when, in the 1920s, the houses on the Lowther estate were under construction large quantities of building materials were brought by water and unloaded here into horse drawn wagons and taken across the surrounding fields.

Windmill Field

The Court Rolls of 1657 and 1664 contain references to 'Windmillfeild' and early maps between 1673 and 1733 mark a windmill symbol near the Thames close to Mill Lodge in Lonsdale Road. Rocque's maps of 1745 and 1762 record 'Windmill Farm' in this area but he also marks the Common mill quite clearly. The churchwardens' accounts at no time indicate that there were two mills in the parish and so this is a subject open to debate.

There is a possibility that at some time before either the sixteenth or seventeenth centuries the Common mill, referred to as early as 1443, fell out of use and was replaced by another close to the river on the Barn Elms Estate. Records state that when Philip Walton came as miller on Mill Hill in 1740 he 'erected a windmill' so it could be argued he re-established an old practice of corn grinding on the Common. Thus Barnes never had two mills simultaneously in operation.

A pencil sketch c1805 is inscribed Barnes Church and shows St. Mary's tower in the distance and a mill in the foreground close to water. As it is a well-known fact that there was much marshy ground on the Common at that date the presence of water does not signify that this mill was near the Thames. It is far more likely to be an illustration of the smock mill erected after the hurricane disaster of 1780 (see section on Mill Hill).

In 1833 rates were paid by George Chapman for Mill Farm and the entry describes the property in some detail but there is no mention of a mill. The likelihood is that the Harrodian Club, which today occupies Mill Lodge, stands on the land of a former mill, in a breezy situation close to the river.

Barnes Follies and Unusual Buildings

Attwell's Folly Professor Henry Attwell ran a private day and boarding school for boys from 1859–1890 in Nassau House, Church Road, facing the Green. On his retirement he moved to a smaller residence which formerly stood on the west side of Nassau Road at the corner of Church Road. The old house and grounds were sold to a local builder, John Norton, who obtained permission to build a row of houses on the site. Certain specifications were required when the Barnes District Local Board approved the plans in January 1894, one being that the basements were not to be more than four feet deep. These houses are Nos. 31–37 Church Road and were immediately nicknamed Attwell's Folly by local residents as they were considered to be too close to the road and likely to be subjected to flooding which in those days frequently occurred in that area after heavy rain storms.

The Tower, The Terrace Until the turn of the century there were two towers at houses along Barnes Terrace. That at St. Ann's was demolished with the house and from the Chinese tea room, on the top floor, the view of the river must have delighted Lord Lonsdale's guests, especially on such occasions as the Oxford and Cambridge boat race.

The second tower still stands and was originally a free- standing building in the grounds of Elm Bank. This house was demolished in 1904 and flats built on the site. An engraving of 1877 shows the house with the tower above the garden trees, although the fenestration of the top storey is different from that of today. This may, of course, simply be artist's licence. It is not know by whom the tower was erected but again the view of the river from the top floor made the ascent, by a narrow wooden staircase, well worthwhile.

Barnes Common Station

The Barnes stationhouse is known for its countryside setting, the yard embowered by the approaching woods and with a remarkable feeling of period in the booking hall entered through a gothic doorway. The walls outside are stoned quoined and diapered with blue bricks. The windows are mullioned, and tall chimneys with hexagonal cannon tops rise above the dormers and steep ridge roof. The wings are later. It can be attributed with near certainty to William Tite (1798–1873) who was knighted in 1869: he designed many stations in the south-west having earlier been a church builder. His distinguished station at Windsor exhibits the Tudoresque gothicism seen at Barnes.

The Richmond Railway minutes have little to say. In March 1846 it was suggested that the station should have tiles instead of slates, with 'chimney pots in character and a small room in the roof'. In April the payment of £11,075 was approved to John Tombs for building the stations both at Barnes and Putney. Putney and Mortlake were much smaller single storey places in the mock affectation of Barnes. Mr. Tombs in January 1847 received a final payment of £500. Meanwhile the Barnes copyholders complained that the station trespassed beyond the boundary of the land allotted to it.

The Lion Houses

This peculiar feature in Barnes is confined to houses in Laurel and Glebe Roads, Hillersdon Avenue and The Crescent, but it is not unique to this area for lions also adorn houses in and around Parson's Green.

These little sandstone lions appear to be the house sign of James Nichols, a builder, who lived in Barnes and had his yard at the end of Willow and Brookwood Avenues, which he also erected in 1906 and 1907. These lions have aroused so much interest that in October 1954 they were the subject of correspondence in *The Times* newspaper and a suggestion that 2,000 were ordered in error instead of two was deemed far-fetched as they were more likely to have been Nichols' trade mark.

Nichols began his house building in Barnes in 1899 when he obtained consent to put up fourteen houses in The Crescent and by 1902 had made a start in Laurel Road. He erected his own home, named The Dolphins, in Hillersdon Avenue but it was demolished after his death and two bungalows (Nos. 17 and 19 Hillersdon Avenue) were built on the site. In the mid 1960s No. 17 was demolished in preference for a small number of flats.

Barnes Common Railway Station – with its mullioned windows, tall chimneys and the pattern of blue bricks – it is an outstanding Folly put to practical use. The later wing unfortunately did not copy the pattern of the original building.

The residents of the Lion Houses are in a conservation area and strict controls have been placed on these friendly looking beasts. They guard the entrance gateways as well as looking down on passers-by from their lofty positions on gables, a height which could not be reached by even a circus trained beast.

The Icehouse, Barn Elms

The Mound, as it is called, by the north-west corner of the anglers' lake, covers the remains of the icehouse which supplied Barn Elms with ice throughout the year, summer and winter for cooling cordials and wine, and for making ice cream and assorted cold relishes. It was a domed circular brick structure under a hillock of earth planted with trees and shrubs for insulation and ornament. When the lake was frozen hard sufficient ice was cut away and harvested, taken by wheelbarrow into the tunnel opening on the west side of the icehouse and tipped down into the ice well below the dome. There was a drain below the ice well to void any water, the great bane of icehouse management, traditionally the province of the head gardener.

The ice would keep for years when properly packed in. Game, poultry, meat, fruit and vegetables out of season were preserved on shelves round the walls above the ice surface. The icehouse appears on an undated plan of c1771. Icehouses were common in England from the previous century but declined with the importation of ice from America and the invention and marketing of industrial ice. In the Ranelagh Club era, at least in 1912, the Barn Elms icehouse, then defunct, was used as a dressing room by actors who performed in the open air theatre by the side of the lake. It is shown on the 1952 25 inch OS as The Mound, with a circular path winding to the top. Having become the haunt of vandals it was regrettably filled in as a dangerous structure.

The Cattle Creep

The bricked up entrance to the cattle creep or 'cattle arch' is found in the retaining wall on the south side of the railway, a few steps from the Vine Road level crossing. It is a low barrel vaulted brick tunnel which allowed cattle grazing on Barnes Common to be driven under the railway without the danger of using the level crossings or straying on the lines. There was no provision for it in the Act of 1845. It appears unnamed on the 1867 OS map. All trace of the entrance on the northern side near the footpath from Barnes Station to Vine Road is obscured by piled earth and close bushes.

The creep was closed by the Army in the Great War, with boarded and locked doors at each end. There remain those who recall exploring it in childhood as a damp and muddy place, too low for adults to walk upright. In 1959 after the creep was discussed at a meeting of Barnes Borough Council a rider attempted without success to take his horse through to prove a point. The entrance to the creep, which contains a large concrete service pipe, was then sealed with a brick wall.

Railway Side and Westfield Allotments. This view was taken from the railway in 1961. The flats were then in the course of construction and the Beehive, with its creepered canopy, is in the centre of the line of cottages.

10. OUTDOOR PURSUITS

Cricket At one time cricket was played on Barnes Green probably between the brook and the pond. At the Annual Vestry Meeting in 1890 it was no longer considered safe to allow adults to play there so it was agreed that money should be granted to make a pitch between Scarth Road and the railway line. The following year, at the Vestry Meeting, the matter was again referred to and it was reported that the work was nearing completion at a cost of £200. Cricket matches on this ground have given continuous pleasure for a century.

Football From the Vestry Minutes, 29 February 1828: 'It having been reported to the Vestry that a nuisance had arisen in the parish from several persons having played football in the street on Shrove Tuesday, which had never occurred before, . . . It was resolved that the Rector and Officers for the time being do take proper steps to prevent a similar nuisance in future.'

From the Vestry Minutes, 16 February 1836: 'It appearing to the Vestry that football being played in the village and the highways of this parish is a dangerous nuisance to inhabitants and persons travelling on the highway . . . It was resolved that the constable and head borough be requested to aid and assist the police if necessary in preventing the game of football being played in public streets and highways of the parish.'

Notwithstanding these unfortunate occurrences football in Barnes has contributed greatly to the national game. Ebenezer Cobb Morley came to Barnes in 1858 at the age of twenty-seven. He and his friends played first on Barnes Green and then the Barnes Football Club was formed and the ground they used was on Limes Field, Mortlake. As there was an absence of rules Morley proposed that they be drawn up and generally accepted. At a meeting in London on 1 December 1863 he drafted the first rules for the Football Association and became its first secretary and second president.

The Barnes Football Club later played on the Cressy House Pitch, Barnes Common. It was dispersed during World War I and reformed in 1926 only to close again during World War II. Since then it has again been revived and uses the ground on Barn Elms playing field.

Other local clubs have been named as Barnes United and Barnes Albion. These played on Mr. Kirk's meadow which is now Watney Road, Mortlake.

The Ivy Football Club played on a Vine Road pitch opposite to the house named Ivy Walls. It was using this now defunct pitch before World War I.

Rowing As Barnes is a waterside village it is only to be expected that rowing should have been accepted as an outside pursuit. The description 'waterman' which frequently occurs in records of wills, etc. refers to an occupation and not a sport and is perpetuated today by the Waterman's Arms on the corner of Lonsdale Road and the High Street.

According to the *History of Barnes* by J.E. Anderson the Barnes and Mortlake Regatta was first rowed in 1840 and became an annual event until 1889. He states that the course was one and a half miles long and stretched from Strand-on-the-Green to a position where the railway bridge crosses from The Terrace to the Chiswick Bank. Anderson lists the winners of the Senior Four-oared Race for a Challenge Cup of £75 in value for the years 1862 to 1888. He further states that by 1879 there was lack of support by spectators and the Maria Wood, which had served as a Grand Stand, was broken up shortly before the turn of the century.

The rowing clubs which competed in this Regatta were those whose boathouses were in nearby vicinities, i.e. Putney, Hammersmith, Isleworth, Twickenham and Kingston, but entries came from further off, for the Fitzgerald Challenge Cup for Public School Fours was won in 1883 by Bedford Grammar School. The White Hart Hotel was undoubtedly the central meeting place for members of the rowing fraternity and one landlord, shortly before the turn of the nineteenth century, was the famous sculler Mr. George Bubear.*

But there was a much greater attraction each year which drew thousands of sightseers to the area, the Oxford and Cambridge Boat Race. It no longer attracts the great crowds of yesteryear but, because of television, has many more spectators. Prior to World War II the local children, for a week or two before the great day, wore light or dark rosettes and shop windows were cleverly dressed out to attract the attention of passers-by. Barnes was *en fete* and thoroughly enjoyed its annual brief moment of fame.

Shooting   The Barnes Rifle Club had a short existence. It was affiliated to the National Rifle Association in 1908 as No. 1414 when it was described as a Miniature Range Club shooting 25 yards with a membership of twenty-two civilians. The Secretary was a resident of Byfeld Gardens and the Club's address was given as the Red Lion. The land used for shooting was in Ferry Road but c1913 the ground, on which the butts were situated, was bought by Mr. Harvey, a local builder, for house development. The Club had already ceased to pay its affiliation fee to the N.R.A. and no further record has come to hand.

Bicycling   In *The Bicycle* for 1876 under the heading 'Country Bicycle Clubs' is recorded: 'Barnes. North Surrey Bicycle Association, Edinburgh Castle Hotel. Secretary Mr. H.A. Barrow, The Ferns.'

In April 1885 there was an annual tricycle meet on Barnes Common. It is recorded 'the 512 cyclers including 41 tandems and 50 ladies rode in procession to the Barnes Common Meet making quite an imposing array as they wheeled two abreast between rows of enthusiastic spectators'.

In 1891 the *Cyclist Year Book*, under the list of Metropolitan Clubs, records that the Barnes Cycling Club had as its headquarters the Lecture Hall in Cleveland Road. The Hon. Secretary was then Mr. W.R. Cotterell of 1 Railway

*Some years back the Barnes and Mortlake History Society was fortunate in acquiring a tankard decorated with an insignia and inscribed 'Barnes and Mortlake Regatta 1867 Scratch Eights'.

Cycling on Barnes Terrace in 1890: These two brothers were members of a large family who lived at one time at the Limes in Mortlake High Street.

Street (now Westfields Avenue) while the Captain was a Mr. O. Paine. A uniform was worn of grey check and the colours are listed as black and red. It was stated that the minutes had been kept since January 1889. The membership appeared to keep around the thirty mark but in 1898 the club stated it was open to ladies.

By 1894 Edward Terry, theatre owner and actor, who lived at The Priory, Church Road, opposite St. Mary's, appears to have been an enthusiast for this sport. He annually presented a cup to the club and a gold medal to the winner of a 52 mile race to Brighton. The dinner, at which the presentation was made, was held at the Holborn Restaurant. The rules laid down were that if the race was won by the same member on three consecutive occasions the cup could be kept by him. There is no record of this happening and it would be interesting to know whether this trophy is still in existence.

On the occasion of Queen Victoria's Diamond Jubilee celebrations an illuminated bicycle procession wound its way across the Green and finished at The Priory. Here Terry's daughters acted as judges. Cycling clubs remained popular until after World War I and during the 1920s the *Barnes and Mortlake Herald* recorded weekend runs by local groups. However, with increased traffic on the roads they gradually went out of fashion and ceased to exist.

Bowls   This is the oldest game to be found among Barnes sport records. The earliest reference is in 1693 to the 'cottage and land called the Bowling Green' and the site was by the Pond where later the school and now the Day Centre is situated. By 1775 the premises were let by the owner, Henry Arthur Hoare of Barn Elms, to the parish as a school room and house for the schoolmaster and the bowling green became a playground and garden.

Fortunately a new site was close at hand just across the village street at the Sun Inn and here for over two centuries the game of Crown bowls has been continually played. There are now a number of other greens where the game is enjoyed and Barnes numbers many keen players among its residents.

Tennis   In the nineteenth century, when there were still many large houses standing in Barnes, this game could be enjoyed privately within their grounds. Photographs have appeared of courts in the gardens of Essex House and Beverley House School and a number of Castelnau houses also had sufficient space for the game to be enjoyed. As the neighbourhood increased in size enthusiasts grew in number and public courts and clubs, with a paying membership, were in demand. The Recreation Ground laid out by the Urban District Council at the turn of the century in Rocks Lane (then called Ranelagh Gardens) made provision for a number of courts which could be booked in advance on application to the groundsman and later, when the Castelnau housing estate had been built some courts were provided in the ground between Washington Road and Barnes Avenue.

Of the private clubs the largest and oldest in Barnes was the Lowther Tennis Club in Ferry Road. Here there were grass and hard courts and an excellent pavilion for social events. This club held an annual summer tournament and had the distinction of numbering Surrey county players on these occasions.

Smaller clubs such as the Vine Cottage Club at the corner of Westwood Road had largely a neighbourhood membership and similar groups of friends formed their private clubs in gardens of sufficient size. One such met for many years during the 1920s and 30s in the garden of 125 Castelnau, the members playing badminton in the winter months in Holy Trinity Parish Room.

Sports Clubs

Ranelagh Club   This most exclusive London sports club was opened in Barnes in 1884. The chief game was polo although tennis, croquet, golf and swimming were also much to the fore. The club played an important part in the early development of flying: the Royal Aero Club used the ground as its main base until 1908 and balloon races from Ranelagh were annual events for a number of years.

But the social side was the *raison d'etre* for the club's existence and, during the summer months, royalty of many nationalities attended the garden parties which were a regular feature. Inside the house the rooms served a variety of purposes as winter garden, dining-room with a musicians' gallery, dance floor, drawing rooms and smoke room. At dinner full evening dress was required to be worn by ladies and gentlemen – white ties and tails *de rigeur*.

The grounds were an added attraction with magnificent trees, sweeping lawns and flower beds. There was an outdoor theatre and on the lake swans, herons, flamingoes and lesser water birds swam among the lilies. It is no wonder that the club was described as 'quite the best equipped and managed of its kind and one of the most favoured resorts that fashion has ever had'.

The Club finally closed in 1939 and during World War II part of the grounds were used by Barnes residents as allotments. The house was destroyed by fire in 1954, although by then it was in a ruinous state, and the area is now used as school playing fields.

Harrodian Sports Club This club was formed for the employees of Harrods Stores in Knightsbridge. In 1880 Mill Lodge had become the home of Mr. Samuel Keene J.P., his wife and innumerable children. After the deaths of Mr. and Mrs. Keene, soon after the turn of the century, the house became the club house and the grounds used for a variety of sports. The land stretched from the house along Lonsdale Road to Verdun Road and then in a southerly direction to Ferry Road. In addition to football, both Rugby and Association, all sports were provided for including swimming in an outdoor pool.

Barnes Sports Club This club was formed in 1920 on former market garden land stretching from Lonsdale to Lowther Roads. There are facilities for cricket, tennis, croquet, bowls and hockey and a large club house is approached from the Lonsdale Road entrance. The official *Barnes Guide* c1930 stated that there were between four and five hundred members.

BIBLIOGRAPHY

Maps and Plans

1649 Survey of the Manor of Barnes
1746 J. Rocque
1783 J. Taylor
1830 Leigh's Panorama of the Thames
1836 Plans of City of London and Richmond Railway
1837 Tithe map of Barnes
1837 London and Richmond Railway plan
1844 Richmond and West End Junction Railway
1849 J. Wyld
Ordnance Survey maps 1865, 1867, 1933, 1952, 1968
1981 Rights of Way. London Borough of Richmond upon Thames

Manuscript and Unpublished Sources

Attwell, Mary Private manuscript memoirs. BMHS
Barnes Census returns 1841–1881
—— Civil rate books
—— Church rate books
—— Court Rolls
—— Land Tax Returns
—— Parish Registers Baptisms, marriages, burials
—— Urban District Council and Borough of Barnes minutes of meetings
School log books: National School on Barnes Green, Westfields School for boys, girls and infants
Waterworks: Minutes of West Middlesex Waterworks Co.
            Metropolitan Board of Works

Periodicals, Newspapers, etc.

Barnes and Mortlake History Society Newsletters
Barnes and Mortlake Herald
Barnes, Mortlake and Sheen Times
Barnes Parish Gazette 1887–1906
The Bicycle 1876
Cyclist Year Book 1891
Illustrated London News
Kelly's Street Directories
London P.O. Directories
Lowndes London Directory 1798
The Times

Printed Material

Anderson J.E. *History of Barnes* 1899 Revised 1983
Anon. *Harrods Estates Offices and Auction Galleries* 1972
Asling E. *The Story of St. Michael and All Angels', Barnes* 1928
Barnes and Mortlake History Society's Publications:
        Barnes and Mortlake As It Was 1977
        Vintage Barnes and Mortlake 1979
        Barnes and Mortlake People 1982
        Barnes and Mortlake Remembered 1988
Baron-Wilson H. *The Life and Correspondence of M.G. Lewis* 1839
Barrett C.J. *The Ranelagh Club, Barn Elms and the Kit Cat Club* 1889
Brewer J.A. *Flora of Surrey* 1863
Brown M. *The Market Gardens of Barnes and Mortlake* 1985
Butler M. *The Barnes Poor House* 1969
Cobbett W. *Rural Rides* 1830
Crimp C and Grimwade M.G. *Milbourne House, Barnes* 1978
Dictionary of National Biography
Farries K.J. and Mason M.T. *The Windmills of Surrey* 1966
FitzGerald C. *Ranelagh and its Times* 1913
Gill R.C. *Street Names of Barnes, Mortlake and East Sheen* 1977
Hailstone C. *Hammersmith Bridge* 1987
Huish R. *Memoirs of the late William Cobbett* 1836
Jesse E. *Gleanings of Natural History* 1842
MacNalty Sir A. *Sir Benjamin Ward Richardson* 1950
Mason F.J. *Life of William Cobbett* 1835
Melville L. *The Life and Letters of William Cobbett* 1912
Papendick Mrs. *Court and Private Life in the Time of Queen Charlotte* 1887
Pepys S. *Diary* 1667
Richardson R. *Local Historian's Encyclopedia* 1974
Stroud D. *George Dance, The Younger* 1971
Tate W.E. *The Parish Chest* 1969
Winch W. *Bits about Barnes* 1894

INDEX